# Samurai Armour

# Samurai Armour

Martin J. Dougherty

Copyright © 2025 Amber Books Ltd

Amber Books Ltd
United House
North Road
London N7 9DP
United Kingdom

www.amberbooks.co.uk
Facebook: amberbooks
YouTube: amberbooksltd
Instagram: amberbooksltd
X(Twitter): @amberbooks

All rights reserved. No part of this work may be reproduced, stored in a retrieval system, or transmitted in any form or by any means, electronic, mechanical, photocopying, recording, or otherwise, without the prior permission of the copyright holder.

ISBN: 978-1-83886-613-6

Editorial, design and picture research: Amber Books Ltd

Printed and bound in China

ABOUT THE AUTHOR:
Martin J. Dougherty is the author of *Ireland: The Emerald Isle*, *Greek Myths* and *Celts*, among many other titles. A former defence consultant, he has written numerous books on history and military history, including *Vikings: A History of the Norse People*, *The Wars of the Roses*, *King Arthur and the Knights of the Round Table* and *Kings & Queens of the Medieval World*.

# Contents

| | | |
|---|---|---|
| Introduction: | The Samurai | 6 |
| Chapter 1: | Historical Context | 22 |
| Chapter 2: | The Evolution of Armour-making in Japan | 72 |
| Chapter 3: | Armour Construction | 90 |
| Chapter 4: | Ancient Samurai Armour (4th–9th centuries) | 134 |
| Chapter 5: | Classical Samurai Armour (10th–15th centuries) | 150 |
| Chapter 6: | Modern Samurai Armour (16th–19th centuries) | 174 |
| Chapter 7: | Famous Samurai of the Sengoku Period | 186 |
| Chapter 8: | Heraldry | 210 |
| INDEX | | 222 |
| IMAGE CREDITS | | 224 |

INTRODUCTION

# The Samurai

MOST PEOPLE have a general impression of the samurai as heroic warriors, governed by a stern code of conduct and self-discipline, who embodied both fighting power and social virtue. This is a reasonable generalization, but like all social groups the samurai evolved over time. They were shaped by the same forces that created other societies worldwide – conflict, economics and a need to govern.

*Opposite: A depiction of the samurai warriors Ichijō Jirō Tadanori and Notonokami Noritsune locked in battle, showing the distinctive costume and weaponry associated with the samurai class.*

The word 'samurai' can be translated as 'those who serve', which is not exactly the same thing as *bushi*, or warrior. The samurai class were a social group who served in a military capacity and were therefore definitely warriors, but for much of Japan's history there were a great many warriors who were not samurai. To a large extent it was service, and therefore being a part of the stable social order, that defined the samurai as more than wielders of weapons.

Disgraced samurai, such as those who had failed to protect their master or who had actively betrayed him, were expected to commit suicide in a particularly unpleasant manner. Ritual self-disembowelment, known as *seppuku*, was the honourable alternative to defeat and the punishment for failure. It may seem incredible that anyone would actually do this, but the ideal pervaded society to the degree that a samurai who did not do the honourable thing would find his life was not worth living. *Seppuku* absolved the samurai of blame and ensured he would not bring

### *BUSHIDŌ* - CODE OF THE SAMURAI

The code of conduct followed by the samurai, which became known as *bushidō*, made them reliable servants and loyal warriors. It was not referred to in this manner until the 16th century and the details varied over time, but what did not change was that a warrior had to be loyal and honourable. Treachery and stealthy murder were as much a part of ancient Japanese politics as anywhere else, making reliable guards and vassals essential.

*Royal envoys deliver instructions to Ako* daimyo *Asano Naganori that he is to commit* seppuku *as punishment for assaulting a fellow court official named Kira Yoshhinaka.*

disgrace upon his family. With such a harsh self-punishment hanging over them, the loyalty of samurai warriors was greatly enhanced.

**The class system in Japan**

The rise of the samurai class to the top of Japanese society was natural. It is common in most cultures for a ruling elite to emerge and for this group to have both military duties and martial prerogatives. It is not unusual that those who risk their lives and engage in hard training to protect a society will want a hand in governing it, and of course those who can fight can take control if they want to. Once in control, limiting the ability of the lower echelons of society to mount a significant challenge greatly assists in maintaining the status quo.

Access to military training is one tool in preserving the social order. A nervous rabble, no matter how well equipped, is unlikely to be able to stand against a seasoned military force. If the rabble also have inferior weaponry and protection, then their fate is sealed. Thus the military elite have tended to rise to the highest social ranks throughout history. There have always been exceptions, but Japanese society was not one of them.

Social stratification had existed for centuries by the beginning of the Edo period (1603–1868) but it was at this time that the rigid class system was implemented in an attempt to stabilize society after decades of civil war. The status of the samurai was confirmed as a governing and military class. The greatest of them, the *daimyo*, were feudal warlords who maintained a body of samurai warriors to enforce their rule.

*The Heiji Rebellion of 1160 was caused by rivalries among powerful samurai clans. It resulted in the destruction of the Sanjo Palace and the imprisonment of the Emperor.*

Konishi Yukinaga (1555–1600) is notable for having refused to commit *seppuku* after defeat. This was due to his religious beliefs as a convert to Christianity.

The economy of Japan was based on rice farming, making farmers the main generators of wealth and naturally the highest of the non-noble classes. Unlike most European societies, farmers ranked above craftsmen, and below craftsmen were the merchants. This concept was based on what each social group produced. Farmers produced rice and were taxed by the samurai class, while craftsmen undertook essential work and made beautiful items that the upper echelons of society desired or even considered necessary to their standard of living. Merchants, who produced nothing, ranked lowest of those within the social order. Some people, such as beggars and religious figures, lay outside the formal hierarchy.

This system was formalized and enforced during the Edo period, but it was based on what had gone before. The earliest samurai were warriors who served feudal lords and were supported by those further down the social order. They became part of the noble or ruling class over time, and their arms and equipment evolved as the nature of warfare and society changed.

*Japanese blade weapons of the 14th century:* katana, wakizashi *and* tanto.

*Warriors under the command of Kusunoki Masashige defend the castle at Akasaka during the Genko War of 1331 to 1333.*

**Samurai weapons and their symbolism**

Popular culture tends to associate the samurai with their swords, notably the long *katana* and shorter *wakizashi*. Worn together, this pair of weapons was known as *daishō*, and the samurai were the only social class permitted to possess them. The katana became the symbol of the samurai warrior to the point where it was said his soul rested within it. However, swords are weapons for personal combat rather than the battlefield.

While the *daishō* was a symbol of authority and also a means of enforcing it, it might well be thought of as belonging to the role of the samurai class as governors – a social tool as much as a weapon. Swords were used on the battlefield of course, but most warriors went into action armed with the bow or the spear – weapons much better suited to large-scale combat.

> ## THE BOW (*YUMI*)
>
> The bow of the samurai was known as the *yumi* and was of asymmetric construction to enable it to be used on horseback. Making such a weapon required a high standard of craftsmanship, and one could only be used effectively after extensive practice. Only a professional military class could afford the time to become proficient and physically capable of wielding such a weapon, to the point that the lifestyle of the samurai warrior became known as 'the way of the bow and the horse'.

The quintessential Japanese spear, or *naginata*, differed from the typical European equivalent in that it had what amounts to a sword blade at its tip. Capable of making slashing attacks as well as thrusting, the *naginata* was a versatile weapon akin to many European pole weapons. Like other characteristically Japanese weapons the *naginata* relied on a slashing cut rather than the powerful impact of a heavy blade. A straight-bladed spear known as a *yari* was also widely used.

Few swords, or weapons with sword-like blades, are heavy enough to chop in the manner of an axe. Instead, they rely on a slicing action. So long as a sharp edge meets the target firmly enough to bite, and remains in contact, the act of drawing the blade through the wound enlarges the hole. In this manner even a relatively light blade can inflict horrific wounds.

The curve on a blade assists the slashing action, but correct edge alignment is essential, as are the body mechanics of the wielder. A tired or poorly trained warrior – or one who has just slightly misjudged the blow – can make what looks like an effective stroke only to find it has failed to put the opponent out of action. Against an unarmoured opponent, almost any contact with the edge of a *katana* or *naginata* is likely to be serious, whereas striking that effective blow against an opponent who is moving and is protected by some form of armour is much more difficult.

*Satsuma no Kami Tadanori was a key figure in the struggles between the Minamoto and Taira clans known as the Genpei War (1180–85).*

**Samurai armour and its symbolism**

The armour of a samurai warrior was a powerful social symbol as well as a means of personal protection. Its design was intended to intimidate enemies and to remind those of lower rank that they were in the presence of someone important. Practically, it was a force-multiplier and a means of protecting the investment of time and training required to produce an effective warrior.

It takes years to develop the skills required to fight effectively, and to gain the experience necessary for good governance as well as warfare.

*A samurai warrior armed with his primary weapon, the bow. His* daisho *(swords) are primarily personal rather than battlefield weapons.*

*'Minamoto no Yoriyoshi Striking a Rock with His Bow to Provide Water for His Troops'
(by Yamagiwa Toshimitsu, late 19th century).*

A young samurai lost in his first battle was a waste of potential, and a seasoned warrior killed by a stray arrow meant that his accumulated wisdom could not be passed on to the next generation. Keeping samurai alive represented more than just self-interest: it was critical to the long-term success of society.

Thus the armour used by the samurai was a symbol of their importance in Japanese society but also a means of perpetuating that society. Armour designs and construction methods changed over time as the samurai mode of warfare developed and new threats emerged. Technology and the availability of materials also played a part in determining the form taken by armour, along with aesthetic preferences and fashions.

*Right: It is usual for the colouring of skirt segments to proceed from light at the top to dark at the bottom, with the pattern repeated on each segment. However, on this 18th century example the skirt segments each have different colour patterns.*

*Above: Late 16th century samurai armour displayed in the traditional manner seated atop its carrying box. This example belonged to Ishida Mitsunari (1559–1600).*

Armour had to balance protection against weight and bulk, but there were other factors too. Cost might not matter much to the uppermost echelons of society, but some members of the samurai class were little better off than the common folk. The time taken to don armour could be critical during a sudden emergency, and of course a warrior's armour had to permit him to carry out whatever motions were required for his chosen mode of fighting and to ride a horse comfortably.

The nature of the threat must also be considered. On the battlefield, arrows and, later, bullets fired from matchlock muskets could nullify many years of training without the samurai even being the

*'Fighting men', print by Utagawa Kunitsuna (1865).*

intended target. Spears and pole weapons were another battlefield threat, and there was always the chance of an assassination attempt made with a knife or improvised weapon. A duel against a trained warrior armed with a katana or other sword was a real possibility.

Different weapons presented different threats. Protection against a slicing blade could be enhanced by the wearer's movement away from the blow, or the threat of his own weapon causing the opponent to rush the stroke or make a suboptimal attempt to land it. Arrows and bullets, on the other hand, concentrated their force at a precise point in a manner that could not realistically be mitigated by evasive footwork or a defensive sword action. There were also times when battlefield armour could not be worn but there was still a threat of attack. Alternative, concealable, protection was required.

*Samurai armour took a variety of forms, all of them complex and imbued with social significance. Merely donning armour was a skill that required training and practice if it were to be worn in a comfortable and effective manner.*

*Three Japanese warriors depicted some time in the 19th century.*

A warrior's armour thus had to be effective against the threats he was likely to face, but it also had to allow freedom of movement and be affordable. It was critical that it was not so complex it took too long to put on, and ideally it needed to be possible to repair and modify the armour. On top of all these factors, the armour had to play a social role. It needed to project authority and status both as a deterrent and a means of intimidating enemies, or be subtle enough to avoid notice and perhaps causing offence.

As warfare in Japan evolved and social change took place, so did the armour of the samurai develop to counter new threats, to meet new requirements and to embrace new construction techniques. Even after modern firearms made traditional armour more or less obsolete it remained a symbol of the ruling class.

CHAPTER 1

# Historical Context

JAPAN IS AN ARCHIPELAGO of over 6,800 islands separated from the continent of Asia by the Sea of Japan. The shortest sea crossing from Asia is the Korea Strait, which is divided into eastern and western channels by the island of Tsushima. It is likely that the first humans entered Japan by this route, around 35,000 years ago. This was around the time of the Last Glacial Maximum, when sea levels were lower and many areas were uninhabitable due to ice sheets or harsh conditions.

*Opposite: Samurai during the Mito rebellion of 1864. By this time firearms made traditional armour obsolete for combat purposes but it remained a powerful social symbol.*

The end of the Ice Age brought with it a rapid retreat of the ice and a rising of sea levels along with climate change in most parts of the world. It was during this period, around 10,000 years ago, that the Jōmon culture emerged. These were a Neolithic people who supported themselves by semi-nomadic hunting and gathering.

**Ancient Japan (10,000 BCE–794 CE)**

The Jōmon period lasted around 10,000 years, during which rising sea levels separated the islands of Shikoku and Kyushu by creating what is now known as the Bungo Channel. Climate change also made food more abundant, allowing greater population growth and enabling communities to remain in one place for longer before seeking new food resources.

After a warm period that saw many communities migrate to higher ground, average temperatures fell until around 1000 BCE, when most

*Both images: Bone (left) and flint (right) arrowheads, Jōmon period (ca. 1000–300 BCE).*

*A Dogu figurine from the late Jōmon period (800 BCE).*

Jōmon communities moved back to the coasts and were incorporating a large amount of seafood in their diet. Mobility between the Japanese islands was certainly possible, and there is evidence of regular trade with what is now Korea.

The Jōmon era came to an end around 1000–300 BCE, largely as a result of falling temperatures, which disrupted the food supply. Rice farming became the main food source and remained so thereafter. The culture that arose from these changes is known as the Yayoi and may have been imported by a new wave of settlers arriving from Korea.

As is often the case, the Yayoi culture is identified by its pottery, which was first discovered in the Tokyo district of that name in the 1880s.

*Ceramics from the Yayoi period reflect Korean influences, and are tailored to the storage of food such as rice, or liquids.*

Yayoi pottery shows a resemblance to contemporary Korean items, suggesting an influence by way of trade. Whether or not this is true, the Yayoi culture was very different to that of the Jōmon period. Rice production necessitated and enabled the construction of permanent settlements, which naturally evolved into clans or proto-states.

It was during the Yayoi period (c.300 BCE–c.300 CE) that the class structure began to emerge. A hunter-gatherer lifestyle cannot support a class of specialists since almost everyone is constantly engaged in food production. A more settled lifestyle allowed surplus food to be stored and traded for goods made by the emerging class of experts. Among these goods were metal weapons and tools, which became more prevalent as metalworking techniques were imported from Asia.

The next cultural era, the Kofun period (c.300–710 CE), is again identified from its pottery. More advanced techniques included the use of a potter's wheel for the first time. These advances were accompanied by a change in burial practices, with increasingly elaborate tombs built for important people. As society became more complex, a ruling class emerged who could afford lavish burial arrangements. Foremost of these were the Yamato clan, who gained control of much of Honshu and Kyushu.

*This fifth century helmet shows Korean or Chinese influences in its construction. Normally battle helmets were made from iron plates, with gilt copper used for ceremonial items. This example, for unknown reasons, has both.*

During the latter half of the Kofun period, Buddhism arrived in Japan and found favour with some clans. This is sometimes known as the Asuka period (538–710 CE), during which the Soga clan rose to pre-eminence and implemented social changes that outlived its period in power. The clan was overthrown in 645 by Prince Nakano Ōe in alliance with Nakatomi Kamatari, but the reforms continued.

Nakano would reign from 662 – though not officially until 668 – to 672 as Emperor Tenji, implementing a series of programmes known as the 'Taika era reforms'. These were intended to centralize power and strengthen the emperor's position as well as setting up more efficient regional governments and taxation systems. The reforms began well enough but Tenji was less successful in overseas adventures. An attempt to resist Chinese incursions into Korea resulted in defeat and withdrawal from the mainland.

BUDDHISM

The arrival and spread of Buddhism in the Asuka period was not without conflict. While Buddhism was compatible with the native religion, Shintō, adherents occasionally found themselves in conflict. Over time, however, Buddhism entered into coexistence with Shintō. In a rare instance of two religions not necessarily being at odds with one another, the native kami – spirits, deities and other objects of veneration – became integrated with Buddhist ideals and figures.

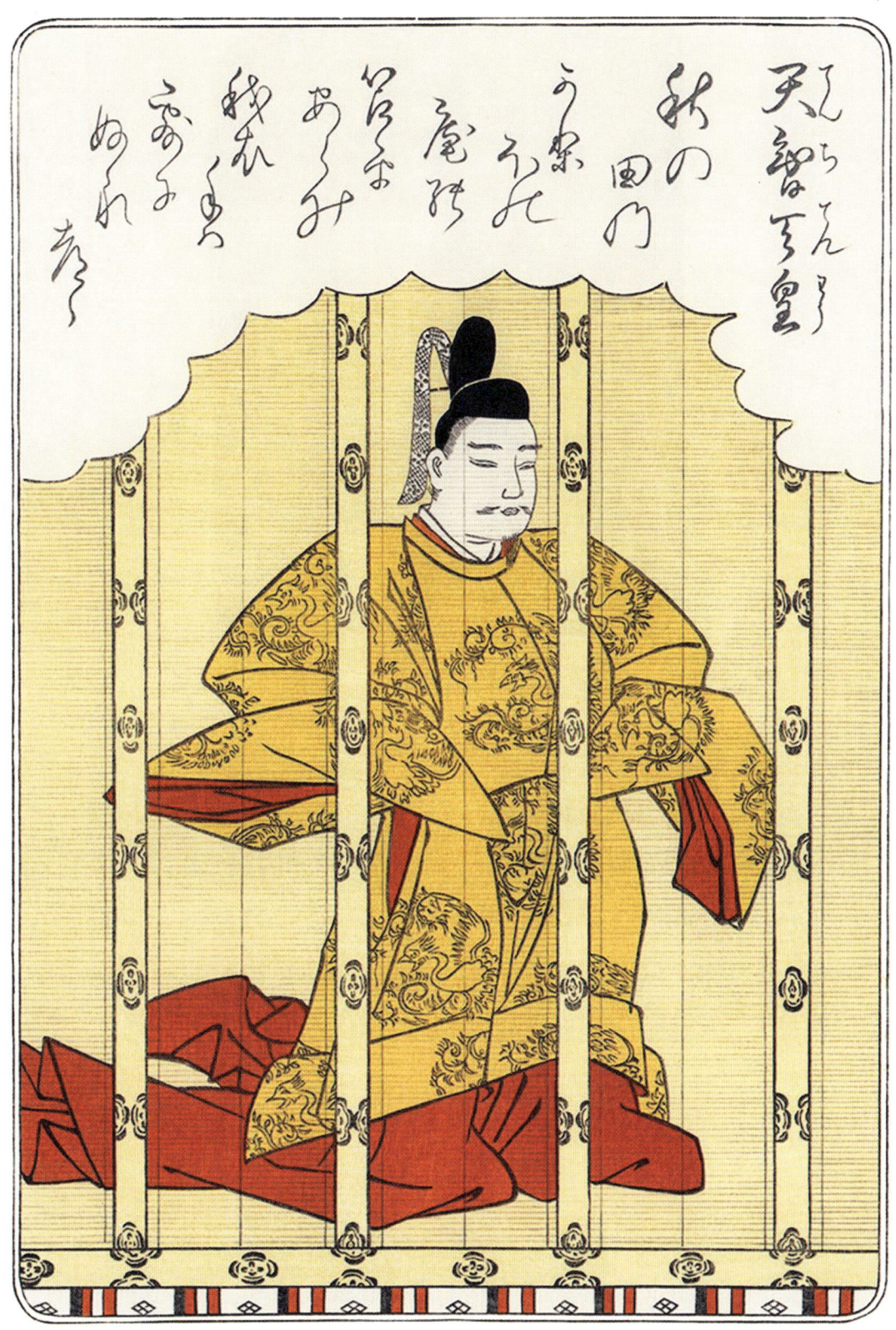

*Emperor Tenji (626–672) was the 38th to reign over Japan.*

*Clay tablets depicting the Buddha were produced in Japan from the mid-late seventh century into the early eighth century.*

By the end of the Kofun period, in 710, Japan had a centralized government and an Imperial palace to house it. Officials were sent to China for training and returned to oversee the new system of land distribution and taxation. Tenji's reforms continued into the Nara period (710–794), though they did not produce the intended results.

### The Heian period (794–1185)

At the beginning of what is now referred to as the Heian period Japan was relatively stable, with a strong central government serving the emperor in a manner heavily influenced by Chinese practice. The Imperial court was moved to Heian-kyō (modern Kyoto) in 794 and was for many years dominated by the Fujiwara clan. Powerful members of the clan married their daughters to Imperial heirs and ensured that new emperors were installed while still children. This allowed the Fujiwara clan to rule as regents, reaching the peak of their power around 1000.

The Imperial court was a centre for refinement and culture, though it was not without internal politics. Later in the period Imperial power was challenged by the rise of great estates (shōen), which were not subject to central taxation. This deprived the Imperial government of funds, which were instead available to ambitious feudal lords. At the same time high taxation forced many poorer farmers to sell their land to those who were better off, further concentrating wealth production among the estate-holders.

*Like many Samurai, Fujiwara no Hidesato was both a warrior and a governor. He served as a* kuge, *or court bureaucrat, in the Heian period.*

*Emperor Saga reigned from 809 to 823, during a time when Japanese culture was heavily influenced by that of China.*

It was in this period that the samurai warrior emerged in a recognizable form. Imperial power had been undermined by the increasing wealth of feudal lords who could raise their own military forces. The breakdown of central authority resulted in or at least permitted more conflict, which in turn weakened the economy and made the possession of military forces necessary. These were, naturally, used to further the interests of the feudal lords in a gradually worsening cycle.

Warriors up to this point were not held in high regard. They were necessary to guard against rival clans and the depredations of other warriors who had turned bandit but were considered – perhaps rightly – to have no cultural virtues. The practice of awarding social rank to those who served honourably resulted in a change in the character of these warriors and thus to the perception of them.

*Led by Minamoto no Yorimitsu, a party of elite samurai battle the mountain demon Shutendoji.*

Those deemed worthy were given social rank and expected to attain at least a degree of refinement to match it, and in an era of decreasing stability membership of a well-armed clan was considered desirable by many warriors. Thus there was a gradual move from rough-and-ready fighting men to an aristocratic warrior elite. This upper echelon of the military class was named samurai, or 'those who serve', reflecting their new respectability. The term was later extended to the whole of the military class.

*In 939, Taira Masakado took advantage of weakening Imperial power to seize control over the Kanto region. He was defeated by his rivals, but the Taira clan continued to increase in power.*

*Taira no Kiyomori was appointed to the post of* dajo-daijin, *or prime minister, for his service against the enemies of the Emperor. Here he is depicted facing ghosts of his victims.*

The Minamoto clan rose to prominence after campaigning on behalf of the emperor, first against Ainu rebels and then the Abe clan in the Former Nine Years' War. This conflict is named for the length of the active hostilities rather than the period between its start in 1051 and the final victory of the Minamoto clan in 1063. The clan became established as a major military power in Japan, whose rise to dominance was made possible by the gradual weakening of Imperial power.

In 1083, the Minamoto clan found itself in dispute with its former allies, the Kiyohara clan. The resulting conflict is known as the Later Three Years' War, again named for the duration of active hostilities. By 1087 Minamoto Yoshiie had crushed all opposition and established himself as a legendary warrior. His clan were now undisputed masters of northern Japan. Perhaps more importantly, they had waged this war

*The riveted plate style helmet (*hoshi-kabuto*) emerged around the 10th–11th centuries (early Heian period) and constitutes the earliest indigenous Japanese helmet form.*

without Imperial sanction, reflecting the new reality where sufficiently powerful lords could more or less do as they pleased.

The decline in Imperial power did not curtail internal politics at the palace. In 1123 Emperor Toba retired but continued to exercise the authority of the emperor in a manner known as *insei* ('cloistered rule'). His son, who took the Imperial name Sutoku, reigned until 1141 despite difficulties caused by Toba. He was succeeded by his younger brother, who became Emperor Konoe. Konoe died in 1155, and Sutoku expected his own son to be selected as the new emperor. Instead, Toba's third son was installed as Go-Shirakawa, much to Sutoku's displeasure.

Toba died in 1156, and Sutoku attempted to usurp the throne in his son's name. He called upon his ally Minamoto Tameyoshi to assist him in seizing the throne. Tameyoshi supplied a force made up of Minamoto clan warriors and some from the Taira clan. The latter had replaced the Fujiwara as the power behind the Imperial throne for some years but more recently they had been eclipsed by the Minamoto. The Taira clan sent a force of their own to oppose Sutoku, led by Taira Kiyomori.

The first clash between the Taira and Minamoto clans, in 1156, was named the Hōgen Disturbance and resulted in a victory for the Taira force. This placed the Taira clan in de facto control of the Imperial government, though their power was challenged in 1159. Known as the Heiji Disturbance, this also was a victory for Taira Kiyomori.

For two decades the Taira clan dominated the Imperial court and thereby held power over most of Japan. Taira Kiyomori's period of ascendancy was known as the 'Rokuhara regime' after his place of

*Demons feature in many tales from the Heian period. Here the demon Ibaraki-doji battles a samurai warrior.*

residence, but upon his death in 1181 the Minamoto clan rebelled once again. This time they were supported by warriors from other provinces. Known collectively as the Genpei War, this conflict from 1180 to 1185 saw the Minamoto clan quickly gain territory and begin an advance on the Imperial capital at Kyoto.

Faced with defeat, the Taira clan fled but were heavily defeated at Ichinotani and again at Yashima Island. The final blow came in 1185 at the sea battle of Dannoura, leaving the Minamoto clan in control of Japan. The emperor was still, in name at least, the supreme ruler of Japan but in reality power was now held by Japan's foremost military leader. This was Minamoto Yoritomo (1147–99), head of the Minamoto clan.

*After Minamoto no Tameyoshi was defeated in the Hogen Distrubance his son was ordered to behead him but refused. Another Minamoto warrior carried out the execution to avoid the disgrace of dying at the hands of the victorious Taira clan.*

*The complex tide patterns of the Kanmon Strait gave the advantage first to the Taira clan then to their enemies, bringing about their decisive defeat at Dannoura in 1185.*

## The Kamakura period (1185–1333)

The title of shogun was originally bestowed upon commanders who were appointed by the emperor and had powers limited solely to military command. Having gained de facto control of Japan, Minamoto Yoritomo took the title for himself and thereby changed its meaning. Henceforth, shogun was a hereditary position of greater importance than that of the emperor. Minamoto Yoritomo's base at Kamakura became the effective capital of Japan and gave its name to the next era of Japanese history.

After the death of Minamoto Yoritomo in 1199, the character of the shogunate changed in a similar manner to the position of the emperor. The Hōjō clan achieved dominance, installing a series of puppet shoguns from behind whom they ruled Japan. The samurai class cemented its power and increased its wealth, implementing advances in agriculture

*Minamoto no Yoritomo reinvented the role of the Shogun as de facto ruler of Japan, with the Emperor as a figurehead.*

and strengthening existing social structures. A recognizable code of *bushidō* began to emerge during this period.

The Kamakura shogunate believed itself strong enough to reject a demand for submission from the Mongol emperor Kublai Khan. This arrived in 1268 and was rejected. Subsequent diplomatic overtures were largely ignored by the shogunate, and in 1274 a fleet of over 800 Mongol vessels landed troops in the most geographically convenient locations. These were the islands of Tsushima and Ike.

Having overcome resistance in these first encounters, the Mongol fleet pressed on to Hakata Bay, where they found the shogun's forces arrayed against them. The resulting battle was a defeat for the shogunate, partly due to superior Mongol numbers and better weaponry and partly because it was an encounter between warriors and soldiers.

> ### DECISIVE BLOW
>
> The samurai possessed better armour than their enemies, on the whole, and their weapons were effective, but they fought as co-operative teams of warriors where their enemies manoeuvred in organized formations. What may have been the most important blow of the battle was struck by a samurai fighting as a mounted archer, when the Mongol general Liu Fuxiang was killed by an arrow. It is possible this is why the victorious Mongols withdrew to their ships the next day, though other motivations have been postulated.

Fortunately for the shogunate, the Mongol fleet was caught by a storm and suffered heavy losses. The invasion force withdrew to Korea and diplomacy was reopened. This was rebuffed in the most graphic manner possible, with the beheadings of the diplomatic parties sent in 1275 and 1279. Meanwhile, the shogunate spent vast sums on defences around Hakata Bay and maintained its forces at high readiness.

The expected attack came in 1281, with over 4,000 ships. Landings at Nagato and Hakata Bay were driven back, thought the Mongol army established island bases and remained combat effective. It was joined by a second large force and renewed the invasion. The issue was in doubt for some time, until the Mongol fleet was again struck by a storm. The surviving ships retired to China and although Kublai Khan continued to press Japan to join his empire there was no further attempt to take it by force.

*Despite outfighting the samurai defenders, the Mongol fleet suffered losses at sea and chose to withdraw.*

*Samurai armour from the era of the Mongol invasions, late 13th century.*

Nevertheless, the Mongol invasion was crippling to the Kamakura shogunate – or rather, the threat of another attack drained its resources to a fatal level. For three decades armies were held ready to resist further aggression, costing more than the shogunate could afford. As stability waned, enemies of the Hōjō clan saw an opportunity to overthrow their control over the Kamakura shogunate. Among them were the emperors of Japan, discontented at being sidelined by a military dictatorship that was itself the puppet of the Hōjō clan.

## The Nanbokucho/Muromachi period (1336–1573)

The system of *insei*, or 'cloistered rule', meant that a child would be placed on the throne at the time when a relatively young emperor abdicated. Former emperors often joined temples, from which they exercised the powers of their theoretically former office. In the meantime, the child-emperor would commonly be controlled by their regent, allowing the regent's clan to exercise political power. Control of the child-emperor was therefore vital to the ambitions of a major clan, and many emperors died under mysterious circumstances as the political winds changed.

With the shogunate similarly reduced to figurehead status, Japan was in a highly unstable position, which was exacerbated by disputes over the Imperial succession. In 1318 the shogunate intervened in the usual quarrelling and insisted that Takaharu, a member of the junior branch of the Imperial family, be installed as emperor.

*Mounted samurai on guard watch during the Mongolian invasion of 1281, from a contemporary hand-painted scroll.*

*Attempting to flee Tokyo, Emperor Go Daigo was captured and sent into exile. It is perhaps a measure of how complex were the politics of the time that he was not simply executed.*

Takaharu took the name Go-Daigo. Go-Daigo had begun plotting to seize power back from the shogunate during his time as crown prince, intending to trigger an uprising when the moment was right. In 1331 his plans were betrayed and, after a period of flight, he was captured and exiled to the Oki islands.

This did not end the conflict, which became known as the Genkō War (1331–3) and was characterized by complex politics and no small amount of treachery.

Ashikaga Takauji, commander of the shogun's main army, was sent to reinforce the defenders of Kyoto but instead decided to join Go-Daigo's followers. The emperor himself had escaped from Oki and had rallied considerable support. At the same time the shogun's regent, Hōjō Takatoki, was trapped in Kamakura when shogunate forces defected and attacked the city. He and his followers committed *seppuku*

rather than be defeated, greatly weakening the Hōjō clan and the shogunate they controlled.

The shogunate was defeated in 1333, and the following year Go-Daigo began attempting to consolidate his rule. In this he was unsuccessful. Warriors who had fought hard for him were dissatisfied by the level of rewards they received, and the emperor was unable to install an effective administration. Disaffection rapidly spread, and in 1336 Ashikaga Takauji betrayed his new master as well by seizing Kyoto.

*The battle of Hyogo (1336) is the subject of many works of art. Some, as here, depict the battle while others show the preparations made by Ashikaga Takauji.*

Go-Daigo retreated to Yoshino and set up his government there. This became known as the Southern Court when a new emperor was installed in Kyoto. Ashikaga Takauji appointed himself shogun in 1338, ruling from the Muromachi district of Kyoto. For this reason the period is sometimes known as the Muromachi period. Conflict between the northern court in Kyoto and the southern court in Yoshino went on for decades, with Kyoto itself violently changing hands and suffering great destruction. Ultimately, the Southern Court was defeated and the two courts were reunited, but the shogunate was once more the dominant political institution in Japan.

The Nanbokucho period is considered to have ended with the reunification of the Imperial courts in 1392, but the renewed shogunate faced the same problems as previous regimes. The Muromachi shogunate was unable to take control of all of Japan, facing resistance from warlords in outlying provinces. Nevertheless, the central provinces were stabilized and the economy benefited from expanded trade with China. Cultural advances were also made, such as the implementation of the tea ceremony.

After a period of stability, the power of the Ashikaga clan started to wane and its supporters began to perceive a chance to elevate themselves. In 1467, a dispute over the succession of a new shogun brought the Yamana and Hosokawa clans, both theoretically loyal to the shogun, into armed conflict. This became known as the Ōnin War and was characterized by bitter street fighting within Kyoto itself, where both clans were based, and by the use of fire weapons imported from China.

Kyoto was wrecked by the fighting, which spread to outlying areas and went on until 1473. Secondary conflict took place between opportunists seeking loot or elevation, and the resulting chaos permitted another social upheaval and the rise of the ji-samurai. These were minor landholders on the fringe of the military class, who formed alliances among themselves and at times clashed with the forces of the emperor or shogun. The term samurai, which originally was reserved for members of

*Right & below:* Yoroi of Ashikaga Takauji (1305–1358). This is a rare example of a medieval yoroi. The yoroi is characterized by a cuirass that wraps around the body and is closed by a separate panel (waidate) on the right side and by a deep four-sided skirt.

aristocratic families and their retainers, gradually came to refer to non-noble warriors as well.

**The Sengoku period (1467–1615)**

The Sengoku period is also known as the Warring States period. It overlaps the Muromachi period, since the Muromachi shogunate was still in place, but was characterized by widespread and often small-scale conflict against the backdrop of a weak shogunate. The feudal lords who emerged from these conflicts became known as *daimyo,* which can be

*The Great Battle of Kawanakajima (1561) was characterized by complex tactics and a personal duel between commanders Takeda Shingen and Uesugi Keushin.*

*In a scene set in snowy hills, the noted Osaka actor Arashi Rikan II (1788–1837) plays a role inspired by the famous medieval warrior and swordsman Miyamoto Musashi (ca. 1584–1645).*

loosely translated as 'great nobility' or 'great names'. Some of the *daimyo* were members of ancient aristocratic families but at this time power rested very much upon the ability to raise and use military force. This enabled leaders of successful forces to ennoble themselves and to take land from those who had previously ruled over them.

Successful *daimyo* passed their holdings on to their descendants, while those who were defeated might be absorbed into these newly emerging noble houses. A form of natural selection gradually reduced the number of *daimyo,* but at the same time the survivors became ever more powerful. That created the need for more soldiers, which was filled by the *ashigaru.*

In both European and Japanese history, much is made of the exploits of warriors of noble name and little is recorded about the

*The* jinbaori, *or surcoat, was worn over armour for protection from the elements. As with other Samurai equipment they were often richly decorated and made from fine fabrics.*

common footsoldier. Epic sword duels between heroes seem to be far more interesting than a determined stand by a group of scared peasants with spears, even though in reality history has been shaped in this manner.

Earlier in Japan's history, *ashigaru* were essentially militia raised – but not necessarily equipped – by a lord to serve in his army. They were not trained and had to obtain their own weapons. As elsewhere

*Konishi Yukinaga was a* daimyō *who served under Toyotomi Hideyoshi. Here he is shown standing over the decapitated heads of his enemies.*

*The Battle of Nagashino (1575) is significant as a turning point in Japanese warfare. Despite a determined siege the greatly superior Takeda army was unable to break through Nagashino castle's defences and were driven off by a relief force equipped with firearms.*

in the world, modified farm tools had to serve for lack of anything better, though successful *ashigaru* might be able to scavenge armour or weaponry. In addition to those ordered from the land, a force might gain some opportunistic *ashigaru* seeking to benefit from a victory.

These mercenaries were anything but reliable and had no loyalty nor anything that would be recognized as social virtue. They were useful for stopping arrows before they hit someone important and for killing other peasants, and of course common soldiers could be put to work as guards and labourers for the army on the march if they stayed around long enough.

When economic conditions were bad, as was often the case in an era of near-constant conflict, a peasant might make a better living from being an *ashigaru* than returning to their farm or trade. There was also the prospect of banditry or extortion, or mercenary work defending

*Okubo Hikozaemon Tadanori carries his lord Tokugawa Ieyasu to safety as their command post comes under heavy attack.*

against other armed bands. This all meant that the *ashigaru* were not well regarded – and most probably did not deserve to be. However, warfare was becoming more complex and was carried out on a larger scale. Effectiveness required organization, and if a *daimyo* was going to invest the food and administrative effort required to march a force over a great distance then he would prefer to get the most out of it.

As a result, the non-noble warriors of Japan became more professional and were given armour and weapons to increase their effectiveness. Accounts of battles still focused on the great deeds of nobles, but the *ashigaru* and other non-noble troops rapidly gained in

*Yamamoto Kansuke was the architect of victory at the hard-fought battle of Kawanakajima.*

# 'SOUTHERN BARBARIANS'

Another great upheaval was caused by the arrival of the so-called 'southern barbarians'. These were actually Portuguese traders who discovered a new market for their goods by accident. In 1543 a vessel was wrecked on the island of Tanegashima after a typhoon, and within a few years Portuguese vessels were calling regularly. Recognizing the potency of the matchlock firearms used by the Portuguese, *daimyo* eagerly purchased them and soon local production facilities were in operation. This necessitated a redesign of personal armour to counter a threat that had not existed a few years previously.

Along with guns came religion, in the form of Christian missionaries. These were initially successful but were soon recognized as a threat to the established social order. In 1587 a decree banned Christians from Japan. It was enforced at most half-heartedly, though persecution occurred from time to time. Christianity eventually became punishable by death, and all foreigners, other than a small Dutch trading enclave, were expelled. In the meantime, Japan began making progress towards unification. This was largely the work of Oda Nobunaga, who captured Kyoto in 1568. The power of the Ashikaga clan was crushed in 1573, a victory made possible to a great degree by skilful handling of troops armed with Western firearms.

importance. High-ranking samurai had to become commanders as well as warriors, enabling them to concentrate fighting power at the decisive point on the battlefield.

**The Edo period (1603–1868)**

Oda Nobunaga (1534–82) rose from a relatively minor military family, establishing himself as a force to be reckoned with by defeating neighbouring lords. He was careful to build a powerful economic base for his campaigns, and to obtain the large numbers of firearms his army would need. In alliance with Tokugawa Ieyasu (1543–1616), he secured Kyoto and installed his favoured candidate, Ashikaga Yoshiteru, as shogun in 1568. His favour only lasted until 1573 when Oda Nobunaga removed Ashikaga Yoshiteru from the position.

This era of Japanese history is sometimes referred to as the Azuchi-Momoyana period after two castles built by Oda Nobunaga. It lasted

*Large arrowheads (Yanone), pierced and elaborately chiseled with landscapes, birds, flowers, dragons and Buddhist divinities, were created to be admired for the beauty of their metalwork a
nd design rather than for use in archery.*

*In later eras, it became popular to create what amounted to 'retro' armour, incorporating features from earlier designs. This 18th century example imitates a* yoroi *of the 13th century. It is characterized by a helmet with prominent rivet heads and a wide, flaring neck guard and by a large cuirass with a separate panel on the right side, large square shoulder guards, and a deep four-sided skirt.*

*The capture of Inabayama castle was made possible by a small party of samurai who scaled the mountain upon which it stood, caused mayhem in the fortress and threw open the gates.*

from 1573 to 1600, while Oda Nobunaga's career came to an end in 1582. Betrayed by one of his vassals, he chose to commit suicide rather than accept defeat. By this time he controlled much of Japan and had thoroughly dismembered the old social order. He was succeeded by Toyotomi Hideyoshi (1537–98), a commoner who won samurai status by exemplary military service.

Toyotomi Hideyoshi continued to attempt the unification of Japan through force. This brought him into conflict with Tokugawa Ieyasu, though after some fighting they became allies. Once in control, Toyotomi Hideyoshi implemented measures to reduce the chance of being overthrown. Non-nobles were forbidden to own weapons and the castles of many *daimyo* were demolished. Invasions of Korea, part of a grand plan to establish an overseas empire, were not successful.

After the death of Hideyoshi in 1598, he was succeeded by his ally Tokugawa Ieyasu, who moved the capital to Edo. *Daimyo* were required

*In battle against Ikko-ikki rebels at Azukizaka in 1564, Tokugawa Ieyasu was reportedly struck by several bullets.*

*The Buddhist deity Fudo Myo-o is depicted on the breastplate and helmet.*

to live there for part of the year and to leave their families at the capital even when returning to their own lands. This large-scale hostage-taking helped deter potential rebels, and the practice of strengthening loyal lords cemented control over the distant provinces.

The class system was formalized and rigidly enforced, excluding commoners from entering the samurai class and tying the peasants to their farms. Economic reform and investment strengthened the economy, which also benefited from a long period of peace and stability. During this time almost all foreigners were expelled from Japan, with trade conducted only through the port of Nagasaki. This was limited to favoured Chinese and Dutch merchants. There is a persistent but unverifiable tale from this period that a duel was fought between a samurai warrior and a Dutch merchant armed with a European rapier. Allegedly, the Dutchman won.

With their islands closed to foreigners from 1633 onwards, and overseas travel almost completely forbidden, Japan entered a long period of isolation. The military strength that had enabled unification now became largely unnecessary, creating a real problem for the samurai class. They were warriors with no wars to fight and needed to justify the stipends they received from the central government.

*After their lord Asano Naganori was ordered to commit* seppuku *for assaulting the court master of ceremonies Kira Yoshhinaka, his 47 samurai retainers did not follow suit. Instead they became* ronin *(lordless samurai), plotting and finally taking vengeance against Kira.*

It was during the Edo period that the samurai reinvented themselves as paragons of culture and virtue. They still trained to fight, but their martial skills were now seen as admirable in and of themselves as well as a means to get a job done. Likewise, the elaborate courtesies and ceremonies connected with almost all activities radiated virtue and generally improved society.

*Right: A 17th century samurai helmet decorated with lacquered wood and metal.*

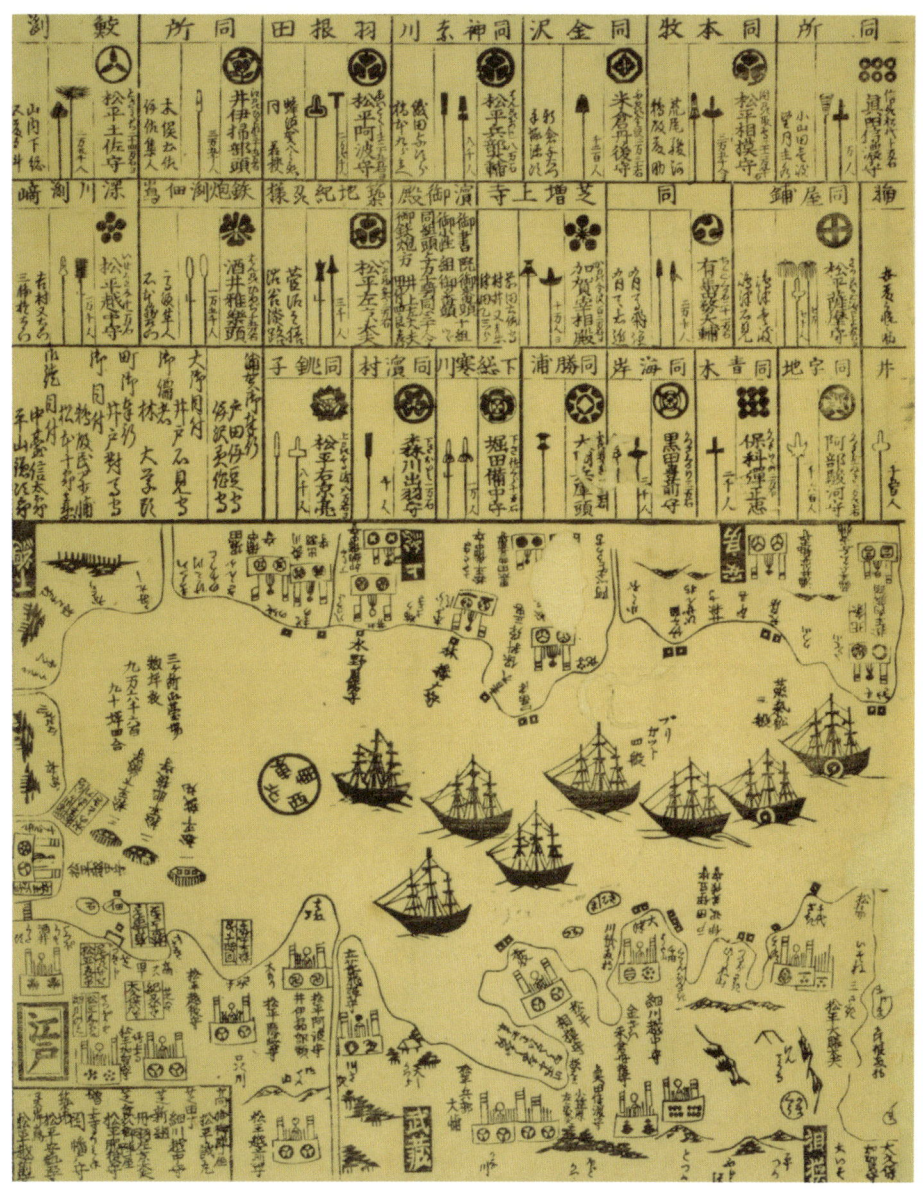

*The arrival of Perry's 'Black Ships' off the coast of Japan in 1853 was a pivotal event, making it clear that the outside world could no longer be ignored.*

Despite this ideal the samurai class had become a drain on the economy. As a well-educated group, they were natural choices for administrative posts but there were only so many jobs that could be usefully assigned. Some samurai families became impoverished, trapped in a lavish lifestyle they could not afford. Disaffection was inevitable.

By the mid-19th century Japan was facing a wave of social discontent, and the 'barbarians' – foreigners – were no longer content to stay away. In 1853 a squadron of 'black ships' powered by steam and under the command of US Commodore Matthew Perry arrived off the coast of Japan. These ships, enormous by Japanese standards and capable of moving against the wind, had come to obtain trading rights with Japan – by force if necessary.

It was immediately and abundantly clear to the Japanese officials who saw them that these vessels were capable of defeating anything sent against them. After a period of fraught diplomacy and some direct threats from the Americans relations were established, after a fashion, and the black ships moved on. Opinions were divided about how to respond. Some *daimyo* were willing to open trade relations while others were firmly opposed, but ultimately a treaty was signed, opening some ports to foreign trade.

This was not to the liking of many *daimyo*, who called for all barbarians to be expelled from Japan. The situation escalated into civil war, and attacks on foreigners resulted in direct intervention from

*The 1868 battle of Toba-Fushimi came about when shogunate forces advanced on Kyoto and were met by the better equipped Imperial army.*

*Modern artillery, such as the rifled, breech-loading Armstrong Gun, added a new dimension to the conflict. Imperial forces also had the latest European and American rifles.*

overseas. Kagoshima and Shimonoseki were bombarded by foreign warships, and imported weapons changed the nature of conflict within Japan.

The shogunate became increasingly discredited and weakened, especially after repeated defeats at the hands of commoners armed and trained by Westerners. In 1868 a group of samurai seized the imperial palace at Kyoto and declared their loyalty to Emperor Meiji. The current shogun, Tokugawa Yoshinobu, attempted to resist for a time but eventually ordered his forces to surrender.

The Imperial capital was moved from Kyoto to Edo, which was renamed Tokyo, and widespread reforms were implemented as Japan sought its place in the new world. These changes were opposed by some members of the samurai class, who unsuccessfully rebelled against the new government in what is known as the Satsuma Rebellion (January–September 1877). Ultimately, however, it was obvious that Japan could no longer remain isolated.

*The forces of the Shogunate were a mix of modern and traditional, with armoured spearmen fighting alongside French-trained riflemen.*

*Imperial victory brought many wavering* daimyos *over to the Emperor's side and put Japan on course to become a progressive, modern nation.*

*Progress was rapid. In 1905 a force of modern battleships and cruisers under Admiral Tōgō Heihachirō defeated the Russian fleet at the Battle of Tsushima.*

Modernization was carried out at a rapid pace, with railways and factories to rival those of any Western nation. By the beginning of the 20th century Japan possessed one of the world's most powerful navies. Under the command of Tōgō Heihachirō, a fleet of modern battleships defeated the Russian Pacific fleet and then a second force sent all the way from the Baltic only to be sunk at the Battle of Tsushima in 1905.

Today, samurai traditions are kept alive by a small but dedicated segment of society who participate in mounted archery contests and other traditional activities, demonstrating the skills of their ancestors as well as trying to personify the virtues they held dear. The code of *bushidō* has found its way to the West with the popularity of Japanese martial arts and Japan has become, somewhat painfully, very much a part of the modern world.

*Edo period samurai armour, combining traditional styling with European influences. Metal breastplates became common after contact with Western traders.*

CHAPTER 2

# The Evolution of Armour-making in Japan

THE DEVELOPMENT of armour design, or indeed any technology, is shaped by factors such as economics and the availability of materials as well as expediency and efficiency. Armour had to be capable of withstanding the threats of its time, and those threats naturally evolved in an effort to defeat it.

*Opposite: Edo period armour worn by Hosokawa Morihisa (1839–1893). The Hosokawa clan sided with the Imperial faction in the civil wars of 1868–69.*

One problem facing weaponsmiths and armour-makers in Japan was the low quality of iron ore available. Iron was introduced into Japan during the Yayoi period, before 250 CE. The vessels of this time were capable of crossing to the mainland and back but could only carry limited amounts of cargo. Imported iron items would therefore have been costly – though in the case of tools and weapons the advantages they conferred were likely worth it. A domestic ironworking industry naturally sprang up once local craftsmen realized what could be done with iron.

*Right: The straight-bladed* ken, *probably derived from Chinese influences, was prevalent until the sixth century when it was supplanted by a single-edged curved design.*

*Above: The* tsuba *provided some protection for the user's hands. The way Japanese weapons were wielded made more elaborate hand protection unsuitable.*

*A* tanko *cuirass from the fifth or sixth century. The* tanko *was the first recognisable 'samurai' style armour.*

Artefacts from this era include arrowheads and tools for the most part, but by the latter part of the Kofun period (around the 6th and 7th centuries) iron weapons and armour components were common. It is notable that the sword today popularly known as the *katana* did not exist at this time, though since katana translates as 'sword', there were certainly weapons of that name in use. Locally made weapons were inferior to those imported from mainland Asia, however, and had a tendency to break or remain bent rather than flexing as a higher-quality weapon would.

One of the reasons for this deficiency was the lack of high-quality iron ore deposits. Instead, metalsmiths had to work with ironsand, which was difficult to smelt and produced low-quality iron. A variant of the bloomery furnace, called *tatara*, was developed to make the process easier, though it remained laborious and required skilled oversight.

Producing iron pieces of uniform quality was difficult, making sword production and similar large-scale projects problematic. However, small iron scales or lamellae were much easier to produce. These could be put together in a manner similar to that used on the Asian mainland to create effective armour.

### *TANKŌ* AND *KEIKŌ* ARMOUR

*Tankō* and *keikō* armour were available in the Kofun period, roughly 300–538 CE, and were made in response to threats from iron-tipped arrows, spears and swords that were in general of low quality. In Europe, the Roman empire had collapsed by the end of this period, and mass migrations of tribes were taking place. The warriors of these tribes fought with axes, spears and swords, and those who could afford it wore shirts of mail. Penetrating these required heavier weapons than were needed to defeat Japanese armour, taking the arms race in a different direction.

*The distinctive design of the curved* katana *blade is optimised for slashing cuts against unarmoured or lightly armoured opponents.*

## Protection from *katana* and arrows

The first known use of the word katana for a sword dates from the Kamakura period (1185–1333), and by this time metalworking had improved to the point where reliable, high-quality swords could be made within Japan. The sword would eventually become the main weapon of samurai warriors, but at this time the bow was their primary armament.

Armour development was guided during this period by the needs of the mounted archer, including survivability. The *ō-yoroi*, or 'great armour', was developed to ward off arrows while the wearer was riding a horse and shooting a bow. Protection against a sword or even a spear was a secondary consideration – mobility was the samurai's best way of dealing with such a threat. As mounted archers had always done, he could ride away from the threat and shoot his enemy as they tried to close with him.

On foot, the samurai wore lighter armour, which was effective against some threats, but could be penetrated by a relatively light weapon,

Katana *with dark brown* saya *(scabbard) with silver dragons and clouds decoration (14th century).*

*Iron plate armour and helmet dating from the Kofun period (300–538 CE).*

such as the emerging katana. Again, mobility contributed to his defence. At this time in Europe, armour was largely dependent on heavy mail, and weapons developed to penetrate it. This again resulted in heavier armour to protect against them. Of course, European warriors were equipping themselves to fight others from the same culture. During the crusades, which were ongoing around this time, some European armour was found lacking when confronted by highly mobile mounted archers who were not willing to close and fight hand-to-hand.

Given the difficulty in producing large pieces of metal armour and the lack of a need to defend against heavy armour-defeating weapons, samurai armour remained relatively light. This is not to say that equivalents of the European pick or mace were unknown, but they never entered widespread use and thus did not trigger a move towards ever-heavier armour. In Europe, this resulted in the development of articulated plate armour whereas in Japan, armour designs evolved but continued to make use of traditional construction.

Early in the Sengoku period (1467–1615), Japanese armour-making was influenced by external threats from the mainland of

*This short sword from the Kofun period would be much easier to make, and less likely to break, than a longer-bladed weapon. Advances in metallurgy and metalworking technique made reliable long-bladed swords a possibility.*

Asia, notably the Mongols and the Chinese and Korean troops their conquests made available. Traditional armour was entirely adequate to counter these threats, so there was no great revolution until Europeans arrived with firearms.

**Protection from firearms**

At the time the samurai first encountered firearms they would have already been familiar with gunpowder weapons. 'Fire lances' may have been in use in China from around 1000 or even earlier. Initially they were nothing more than a quantity of gunpowder contained in a tube on a pole, relying on the jet of flame and hot gas from ignition to cause harm at very short range. Packing the tube with pebbles or other small projectiles increased the effect of these weapons but they were clumsy, unreliable and not all that effective. Samurai warriors can be forgiven for discounting them as much of a threat.

*The* tachi *has a longer and more steeply curved blade than the* katana, *suiting it well to mounted combat.*

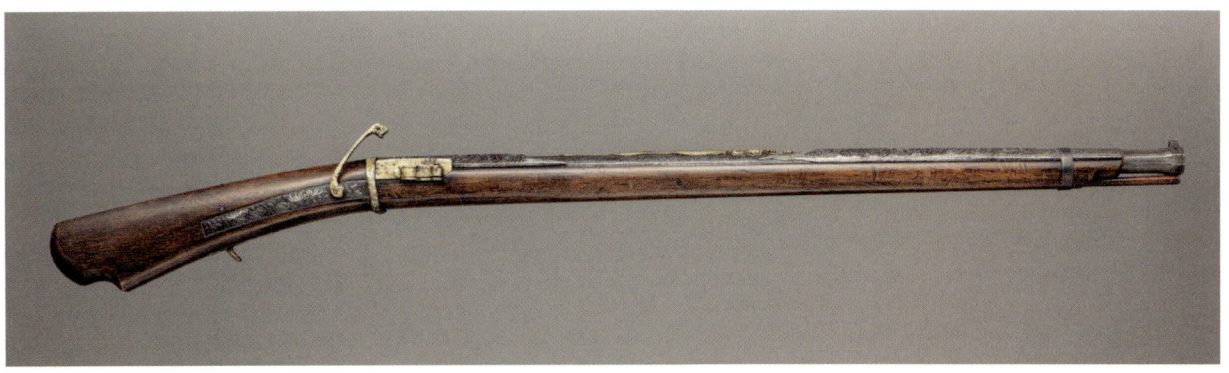

*Matchlock guns were crude, inaccurate and not very reliable. However, they permitted troops with little training to deliver massed and rather indiscriminate fire.*

The matchlock guns introduced by the Portuguese were another matter altogether. Much more reliable, they were also more accurate and hit a lot harder. Rather than a jet of hot gas and some pebbles, the target now faced a heavy bullet that could punch through armour or a helmet. Even if the wound was survivable, bullets greased with animal fat, carrying gunpowder residue and fragments of cloth into the wound, created a high likelihood of infection.

The use of silk under armour benefited the samurai here. If the silk was dragged into the wound rather than being penetrated, it acted as a barrier that not only made bullet extraction much easier, but also prevented debris being left behind to cause infection. Despite this, and the fact that traditional armour could deflect or stop a spent bullet, a need for better protection was perceived.

Japanese armour-makers had no experience of dealing with such threats, nor of making armour pieces that could. However, the newcomers did. Copies of the 'barbarians' armour began to appear, along with experimental versions of traditional armour. It was certainly possible to make armour thick enough to defeat a mid-1500s projectile. Indeed, Japanese armour of the period shows the same 'proving' marks European equivalents did. A wise warrior would not accept a breastplate that had not demonstrated it could withstand a test shot with a firearm. However, full-body coverage was impractical.

*To the Portuguese merchants who arrived in the 1600s, Japan was an untapped mercantile opportunity. Many samurai resented these foreign barbarians and their strange new ideas, fearing social upheaval.*

## HYBRID ARMOUR

As the Europeans found, armour heavy enough to stop bullets had to be produced with advanced articulation techniques. It was too heavy to permit the traditional fighting style of the samurai warrior, and also vastly expensive. Those who could afford armour sufficient to stop bullets had to be satisfied with a breastplate that could protect their vital organs, and a strengthened helmet. The head and torso were the likely impact points anyway, and a hit elsewhere was probably survivable. The result was a great number of hybrid Japanese/European-influenced armours. Some were strange and rather unappealing from an aesthetic point of view, which detracted from the armour's other function as a status symbol. Others successfully integrated European components with traditional design and retained a quintessentially Japanese flavour.

For the next century Japan faced the same influence on its armour design that Europeans did. Guns became more powerful, reliable and accurate, and defeating their projectiles became increasingly difficult. The articulated plate of Europe was replaced by an 'all-or-nothing' style of breastplate, helmet and lighter protection elsewhere. The European 'buff coat' of thick leather could actually stop a pistol or musket ball at moderate range but was not sufficient to rely upon entirely. Japanese armour production followed a similar model, with lighter traditional elements providing some protection to the limbs. What is different is that high-end European armour went from being extremely heavy to much lighter due to the influence of firearms, whereas Japanese body armour became heavier. Both were responding to a set of influences that were now universal.

The Edo period (1603–1868) did not remove these threats, but the long period of peace did mean they were less likely to be faced. Armour became important for its social implications and could follow aesthetic trends more closely. By the time Japan was reopened and 19th-century

*Nimai-Dō Gusoku armour, late 16th–early 17th century. With its striking red colour, the armour belongs to a style that is referred to as Akazonae (lit. "red arms"). Akazonae was a troop formation that emerged in the 16th century, of which all members were entirely clad in red.*

*The* Do-maru, *or 'body wrap', afforded the user much greater freedom of movement than the* O-yoroi, *which was optimized for horseback archery.*

*The Satsuma Rebellion of 1877 represented an attempt to return to the 'good old days' in which samurai were essential to society. It ended, predictably, in defeat.*

firearms arrived, those with experience of them – the Europeans and the Americans who forced the reopening – had discarded armour as more or less useless.

The last hurrah of the traditional samurai, during the Satsuma Rebellion of 1877, demonstrated that traditional body armour was merely an encumbrance on the modern battlefield. Within a century new forms of personal protection would appear, bearing little resemblance to traditional samurai armour.

It can be argued that the evolution of European armour was driven by the development of firearms, whereas the development of samurai armour was driven by their absence. This is a little simplistic, as many other factors were at play. The inability to import good-quality iron ore for much of Japan's history was one, which in turn led to a lack of a need to counter heavier weapons designed to defeat thicker armour.

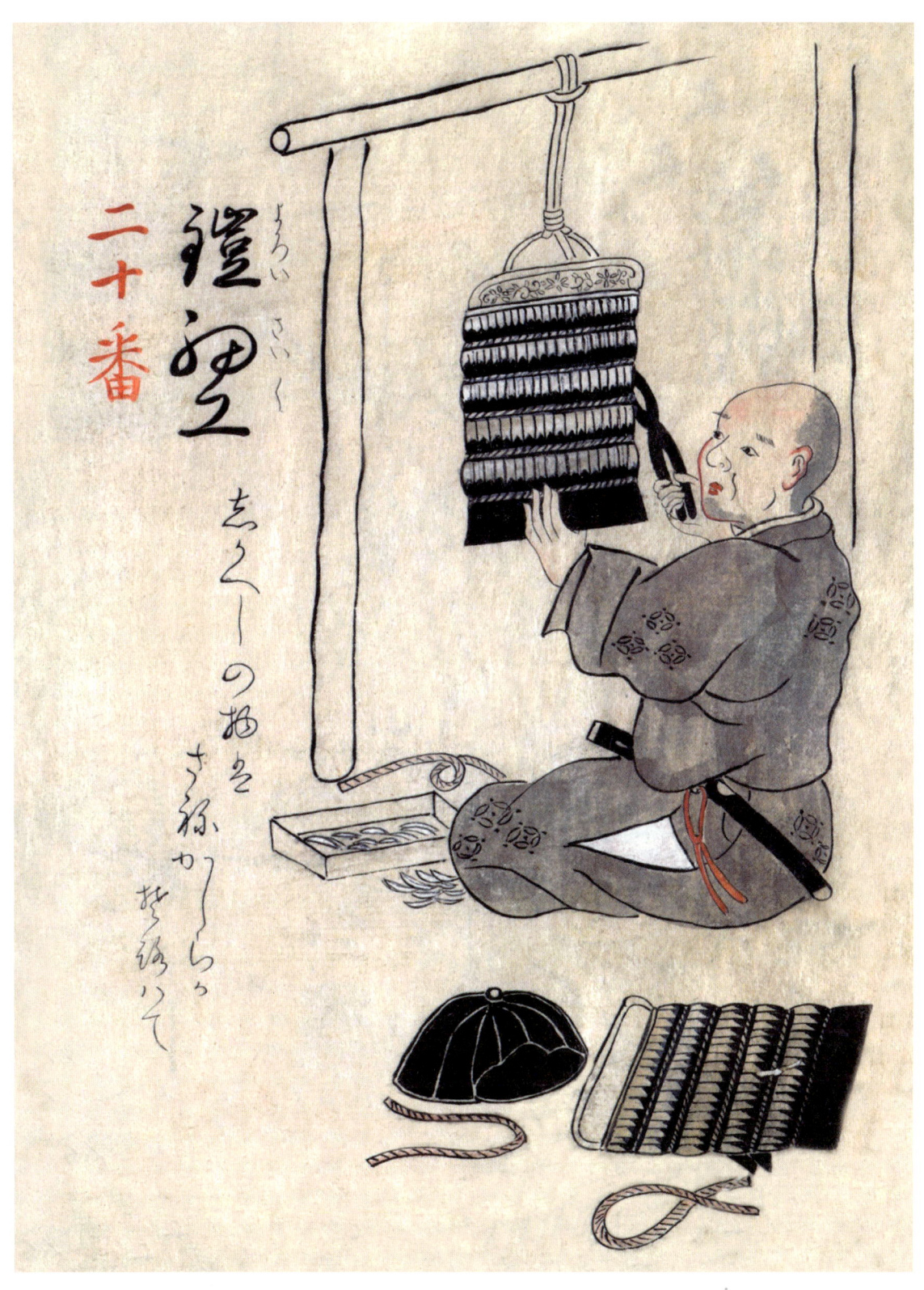

*A craftsman making armour from rawhide, from an 18th century collection of traditional crafts and trades.*

*Entitled 'Actor in Samurai Armour', this 1870s depiction captures the exquisite craftsmanship of Japanese armour making.*

As a result of these factors, Japan's arms/armour race took an entirely different path to that in Europe and elsewhere. This in turn influenced the mode of warfare and personal fighting styles. The iconic *katana* would likely not have developed as it did if the intended targets were armoured in heavy mail or carrying shields. This might have influenced the development of the code of *bushidō* or the nature of the samurai – whose values shaped Japanese society. Traditional samurai armour was therefore not only a symbol of this society but a powerful factor in shaping it.

*Nakazō I Nakamura was a highly influential actor in the traditional Kabuki theatre. Numerous art pieces exist of him playing samurai roles.*

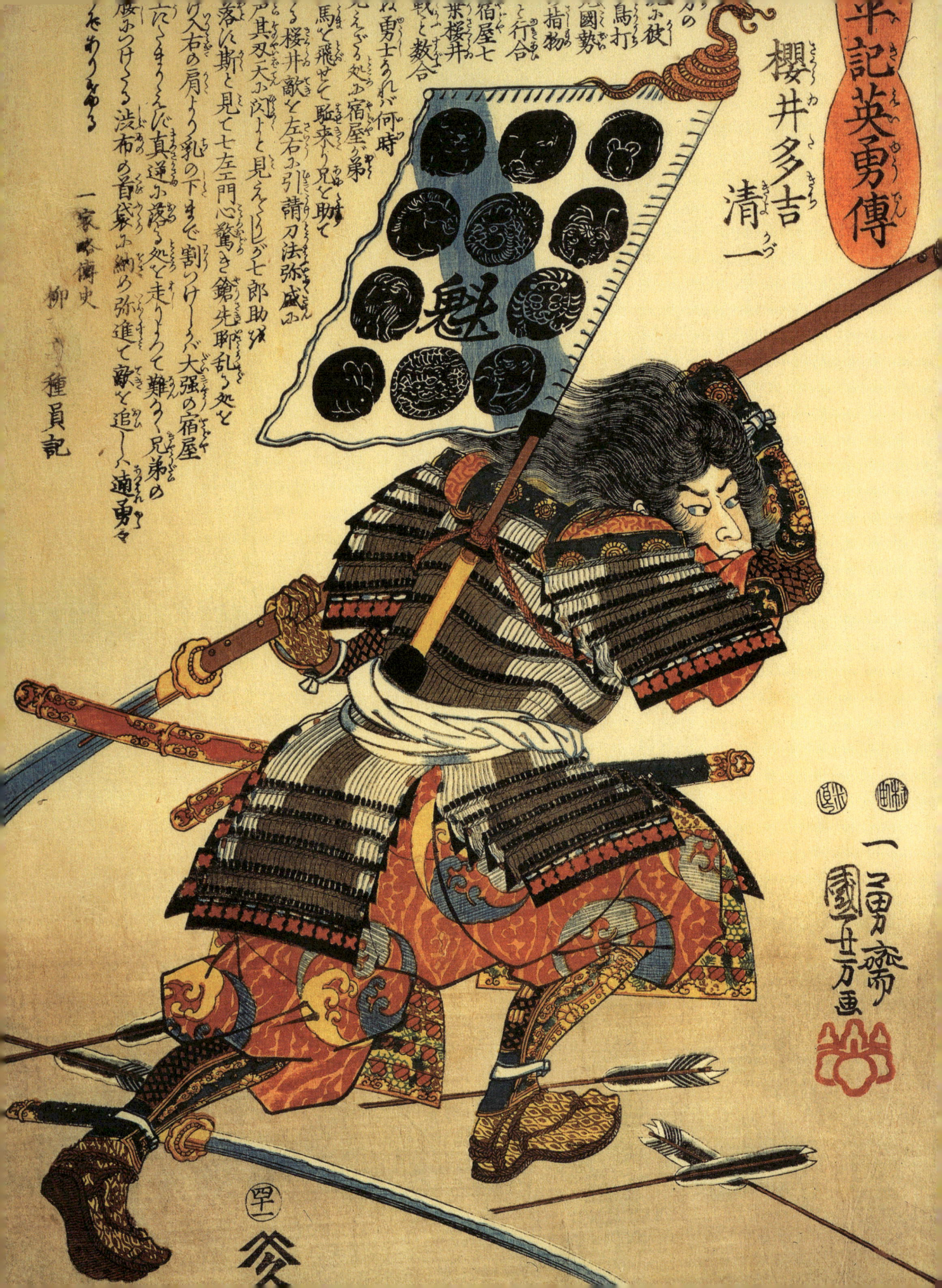

CHAPTER 3

# Armour Construction

JAPANESE ARMOUR is generally classified into three groups. Types used before the 10th century are known as 'ancient armours'. Relatively few examples survive, but those that do are similar to armour types used on the mainland so were likely either copied or influenced, or possibly traded for. Both scale and lamellar construction was used in their production, but lamellar construction seems to have fallen out of favour by the classical period of Japanese armour-making.

*Opposite: Sakuri Takichi Kiyokazu, armed with a* naginata *and displaying a banner on his back, circa 1848–49.*

*Tanko armour of the Kofun period (300–530 AD), on display in New York. Surviving pieces are very rare, with some declared to be national treasures.*

'Classical armours' are usually of scale construction and include all components normally associated with samurai armour. The classical armour period runs from the 10th century until the 15th. From the 16th century onwards, armour is classified as 'modern'. Solid plate appeared at this time, as a result of contact with Westerners. Lamellar construction gained in popularity during this period, and armour in general became more diverse in construction and style. Many components were lacquered, making them waterproof as well as decorative.

*Iron plate armour and helmet of the Kofun period.*

**Materials and their functions**

The armour used by samurai warriors was made out of the same materials used elsewhere in the world, notably iron and animal hide, though construction methods differed. It was not made in large pieces but was instead constructed from small overlapping scales or lamellae. *Kozan-dō*, or scale armour, was produced by lacing together small plates known as *kozane*. Lacing was also used in lamellar armour, though riveting might be substituted. Armour pieces were held together with woven cords. Each piece of armour was separately constructed and could be substituted if it was damaged or if it no longer fitted.

Both scale and lamellar construction used small overlapping pieces of metal or leather. Two types of scale were commonly used: hon *kozane* overlap for about half to two-thirds of their width whereas iyo zane overlap only a little around the edges. This produces armour that

*According to legend, the female samurai (onna-bugeisha) Tomoe Gozen commanded a force of warriors at the battle of Awazu no Hara in 1184. She slew Uchida Ieyoshi in single combat and escaped her force's defeat.*

*A samurai of the Heian period (794–1186) wearing* O-yoroi *armour and armed with a tall, asymmetric bow.*

is cheaper and lighter, but also less protective. It was not uncommon to alternate metal and rawhide scales as a weight-saving measure.

Scales varied in size and shape according to where in the piece of armour they were located and what body part they protected, and overall there was a trend over time towards smaller scales. This increased weight and the time required to produce a suit of armour. Lacquering practice also appears to have changed over time. Early armour was lacquered after completion, but later practice was to lacquer scales individually before assembly. Once lacquered, a piece of armour became rigid enough to give the impression of being a solid metal plate.

Lamellar construction was broadly similar to scale. The main difference between scale and lamellar armour is that scales are attached to a backing whereas lamellae are connected to one another and can form a complete piece without a backing. Some later armours used a mix of the two methods.

*The* Haramaki, *or 'belly-wrap', provided reasonable protection with less weight and cost than the* O-yoroi. *It was used by common footsoldiers as well as samurai.*

# THE USES OF SILK

Silk was also widely used in connection with armour, not only for its comfort and aesthetics, but also due to its resilience. Silk offered a number of protective advantages over other cloth types. It is relatively difficult to cut or pierce, to the point where early experiments with modern body armour started with observations that silk handkerchiefs and garments seemed resistant to bullets in a way that other clothing was not. Silk as armour was certainly known in Asia, with the Mongols as noted users.

It is questionable whether a silk garment could be made thick enough to properly protect against swords and spears without being enormously bulky but any protection is better than no protection. A marginal hit might be mitigated to the point where it became trivial, and even a more serious blow could become survivable.

Even where penetration occurred the silk might be dragged into the wound, plugging it to reduce bleeding and making it relatively easy to extract a projectile. This also improved survival rates by ensuring no debris was left in the wound – infection resulting from scraps of cloth or dirt left behind have killed a great many people whose wounds themselves were treatable.

Silk garments might offer some protection in situations where other armour could not be worn and were socially acceptable. Modern examples include the silk scarves affected by some cultures, which can protect the neck from a sudden slashing attack but are socially acceptable as part of a sharp outfit. As part of a piece of armour, silk improved comfort and added a last line of defence against a weapon that had only just penetrated the outer layers of the armour.

Leather, in the form of rawhide, was a key component in armour-making. It was prepared by taking an animal hide and scraping away all flesh, fat and hair from it, without any tanning process, and was then

*Armour is designed to protect against weapons rather than the elements. Samurai used a surcoat, or* Jinbaori, *for warmth and as a status symbol.*

*A 17th century* Jinbaori *incorporating lacquered wood as well as fine silk.*

worked into whatever shape was desired. Rawhide shrinks and hardens as it dries out, creating a resilient material that has been used for cords, containers and clothing since ancient times. It is lighter than metal but suffers from the drawback that it will soften if it becomes wet.

Ironworking was a mature technology in Japan by the time the samurai emerged as a social class, and techniques continued to improve. Iron was widely used for armour production, but composite scales of iron and steel offered significant advantages. A plate formed from an outer layer of hard steel and an inner layer of more flexible iron provided better protection than one or the other, though this increased the complexity of the armour and difficulty of its production. Despite

Manju no wa *could be worn under the cuirass or dispensed with, depending on the wearer's preferences.*

*An armoured vest, or* Manchira, *to be worn over other armour for additional protection or as a decorative item.*

widespread belief there is no evidence of bamboo or wood being used in samurai armour.

Armour was usually densely laced with silk or leather using a technique called *kebiki odoshi*, creating a pattern that resembles feathers. Vertically oriented lacing was named *tatetori odoshi* while a diagonal pattern was called *nawame odoshi*. Dense lacing was strong but required

# CORDS (ODOSHI-GE)

The most important component of samurai armour were cords, known as *odoshi-ge*. These were carefully prepared from braided cotton, hemp or silk, and were craft items in their own right. Preparation of the great many cords that would be required was a lengthy part of armour construction, but an essential one. Cords were also important in connecting armour components and ensuring they sat properly.

*Scales such as these were a fundamental armour component. The many cords used to tie them in place added to the weight of the armour.*

*The use of separate shoulder guards greatly simplified the problem of protecting against downward blows without requiring complex articulation.*

a great deal of cord, which contributed to both weight and expense. Damaged lacing – perhaps due to receiving blows from sharp weapons – required considerable time and effort to repair.

The construction of each armour part was important, but how they worked together was vital to effectiveness. Well-fitted armour feels 'not so much heavy as tiring' to wear, in that each movement requires more energy than normal but is not restricted to any great degree. Ill-fitting armour, on the other hand, is both tiring and encumbering. Many types of armour place much of their weight on the shoulders and hips. In the short term poorly balanced armour causes the user to tire quickly, and long-term back and hip problems are likely. This can be mitigated, though not entirely eliminated, by good design and fit.

There are six main components in a suit of samurai armour, collectively referred to as *hei-no-rokugu* or more simply as *rokugu*. These corresponded to the location they protected: head, face, body, arms, upper and lower legs. Additional elements are associated with some of the components. Depending on circumstances, some elements might not be worn when undertaking certain tasks. For example, scaling obstacles to assault a fortress might require greater mobility and less weight than fighting on level ground, making it necessary to omit some parts of the armour.

This method of armour construction offered many advantages in terms of flexibility and lightness, but just putting it on was a skill that had to be taught. The exact method varied from clan to clan and over time, and was considered a military secret. An untrained peasant who scavenged armour from a battlefield might find it useless even if he were willing to risk getting caught with it.

*In Japanese folklore the warrior monk Benkei confronts Yoshitsune, intending to defeat him and take his sword to become part of a suit of armour.*

*Helmet belonging to Ashikaga Takauji (1305–1358), founder of the Ashikaga shogunate.*

**Head and neck protection**

Head protection was provided by the helmet, or *kabuto*, and face mask (*men yoroi/ menpo*). The helmet was usually formed from several shaped plates, though some designs were of a single piece. The bowl, or *hachi*, was shaped to deflect a blow or projectile rather than absorbing its full impact. Not only does deflection reduce the amount of force the helmet's materials must resist, but it also mitigates the effect on the wearer.

Projectiles such as arrows and, later, bullets, penetrate best when they strike perpendicular to an armoured surface. In this case the projectile dumps all of its kinetic energy into the target, whereas one that skips off retains some of its energy – which means the target does not receive it. Striking at an angle also increases the effective depth of protection a weapon has to penetrate.

Much the same thing happens with blows from hand weapons. A hard outer surface might deflect a blow and thus not have to resist all

*The wide helmet of this early-mid 14th century armour provides protection against overhead blows and arrows coming in on a downward trajectory.*

of its energy, whereas an edge that bites into softer material creates a guide for its remaining force. Even if the stroke does not penetrate all the way through armour it might cause the target to stagger, becoming vulnerable to a follow-up. This is particularly important in the case of a helmet, as non-penetrating blows to the head may cause disorientation or even unconsciousness.

The relatively fragile neck can also be damaged by an impact to the head, and is difficult to armour sufficiently well to protect against being struck directly. Samurai armour solved this problem with the *shikoro*, which projected from the back and sides of the helmet. It was effective against projectiles and the typical downward or diagonal-downward stroke of a sword.

*Stylised helmet decoration was a way of ensuring a warrior's deeds on the battlefield were noticed and correctly attributed. As armies became larger, identification of leaders and allies became ever more important, giving decoration a command function as well.*

As cavalry became more prevalent the *shikoro* became even more important, as downward strokes were not only more common but also more powerful. The bowl of the helmet and the projecting *shikoro* might redirect an overhead blow past the shoulders, preventing an impact that might punch through armour or break the collarbone. This would render the target more or less defenceless and unable to use his weapons, even without causing a penetrating injury.

There are always trade-offs when creating armour. An enclosed helm offered good protection, but at the cost of limited vision and oxygen supply. Already claustrophobic, such a helm can become unbearable due to carbon dioxide build-up from the wearer's breathing. Small holes do not fully allow expelled breath to move away from the face, meaning the warrior is breathing some of the same air back in. Over time this can become significant.

### FACE MASK

The face mask, or *men yoroi*, might or might not have an attached throat protector. If not, throat armour (*shikoru*) could still be worn even if the samurai chose to dispense with the mask. The Japanese attitude towards face protection differs considerably from European ideas. While open-face helmets were standard in Europe until the 12th century, after this there was movement towards encasing the entire head in thick armour. Samurai face protection was much lighter, if worn at all.

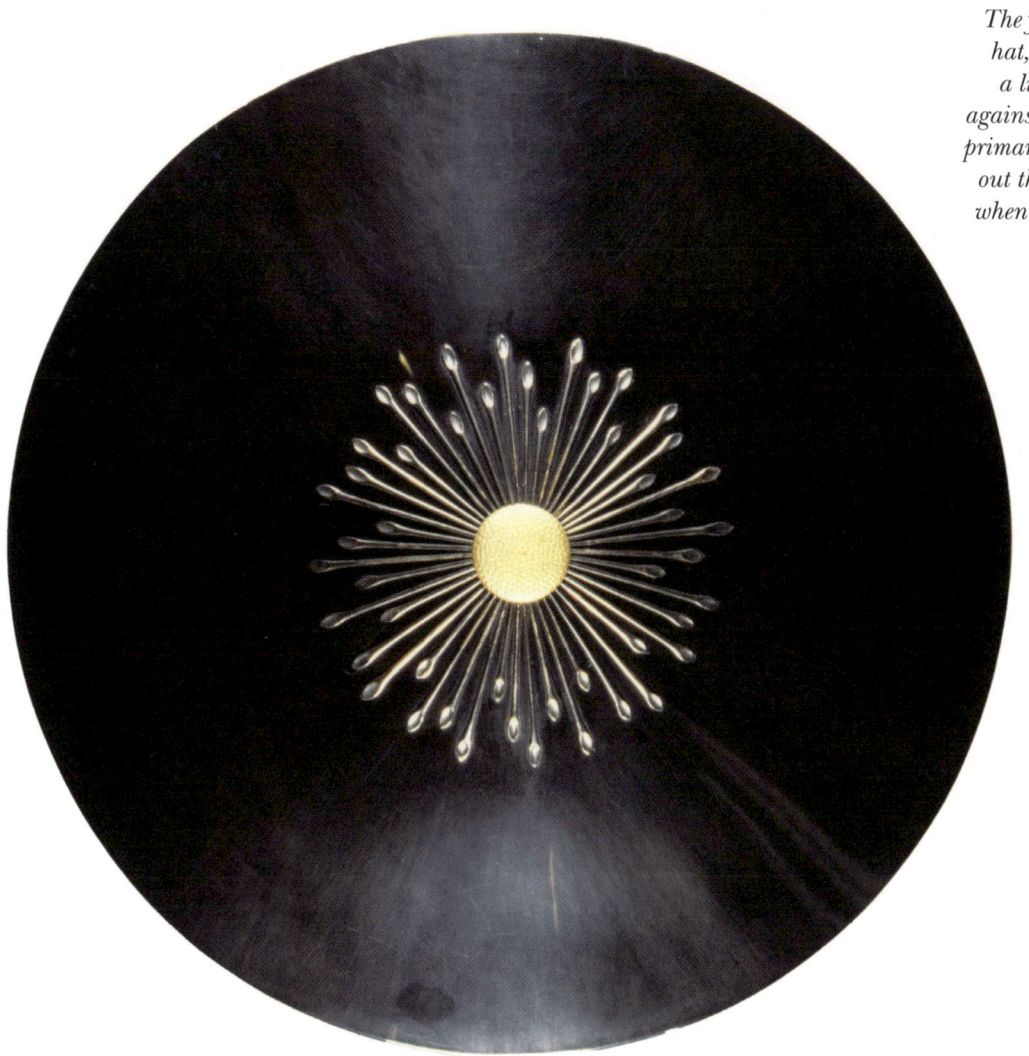

*The jingata, or war hat, might provide a little protection against weapons but its primary use was to keep out the sun and rain when not in a combat situation.*

The helmet and mask, two major elements of the samurai's armour, offered better vision and easier breathing than a fully enclosed helm, though at the cost of increased chance of an arrow in the face. This was reduced by the *mabizashi*, a visor-like plate angled out over the eyes. In addition to resisting a strike to the forehead it would prevent a spent blow dropping across the user's face. The design of the *kabuto* was also intentionally fearsome, impressing everyone nearby with the samurai's importance and the foolishness of fighting him.

*The face mask provided more than one form of protection. It might physically keep out a blow but could also intimidate an enemy into hesitating to strike one.*

The helmet might also carry the *datemono* (crest) or various decorative objects known as *wakidate*. Various designs existed, with different terms according to where they attached to the helmet. Initially, only high-ranking samurai wore a crest, enabling them to act as a rallying point for friendly troops and ensuring nearby warriors understood that the individual bellowing orders at them was doing so from a position of authority rather than overenthusiasm. Later, as force sizes became larger and actions more complex, the use of datemono by ordinary samurai became more common as a way to identify who was an enemy and who was not.

**Torso protection**

Body protection was provided by the *dō*, which translates – perhaps confusingly – as 'breastplate' or 'cuirass'. To Western ears this has connotations of a single solid chestpiece, but that is not the case. Most *dō* were constructed from small scales or vertical lamellae, which might be of rawhide or metal.

*Crests were commonly made from fragile materials such as paper mâché, and might not survive a battle. Returning with a smashed-in helmet crest was a sure sign the samurai had been in the thick of the fighting.*

*An early 19th century cuirass with attached tassets (kusazuri) to protect the groin and upper legs.*

Numerous specific terms existed for the *dō*, each describing a particular combination of construction method, material, and configuration. Not all elements were present in some periods. For instance, in the Heian period (794–1185) samurai armour provided only head and body protection, with other elements added later.

The construction of a *dō* varied considerably over time, and naturally there are technical terms for the many different ways the cuirass can be constructed. The cheapest form of armour was tatami *dō*, which consisted of small plates or scales fixed to a flexible backing. Upmarket versions of *tatami dō* used mail to connect the plates and give better protection.

The design of the *dō* was a complex business, since the human body is not built in a manner convenient for armour-makers. A *dō* had to allow

*An 18th century breastplate depicting Hachiman, god of war.*

sufficient freedom of movement that the wearer could fight effectively, notably allowing arm mobility as well as bending and twisting at the waist. Rigid armour might or might not offer better protection against certain threats but without complex articulation it was not practical for many purposes.

There was also the question of what threats were likely. Blows are more likely to fall on the head, shoulders and arms in close-quarters combat such as a sword duel, so perhaps it might be better to protect these at the expense of the torso. This approach was used in some European societies, with an extended hood of mail covering the shoulders as well and offering excellent protection at a fraction of the cost and weight of full body protection.

*This Chinese armour from the 13th or 14th century shows distinct similarities with Japanese construction and lacquering techniques.*

*Armour of the Edo period, belonging to the Owari Tokugawa clan.*

This method worked particularly well in conjunction with a shield, but the samurai did not make much use of them. Shields were employed mainly as portable fortifications for archers rather than being considered part of the samurai's personal protection. Leaving the body unprotected was not an option, especially since arrows and other projectiles are far more likely to hit the centre of mass than a relatively small arm.

The solution was to add components associated with the *dō* but

Tatami *armour from the Edo period. Armour of this construction was cheaper and easier to construct and to transport, as it folded up rather than needing a bulky carrying box.*

*Haramaki-dō from the 15th or 16th century. This armour opened at the back, ensuring the relatively weak fastening points would not face an enemy's weapon so long as the wearer stood firm.*

not part of it, connected in a way that allowed movement but left few lightly protected gaps. The *sode,* or shoulder shields, were associated with the *dō* but attached to it rather than being part of it. They operated with the *shikoro* as an outer layer of defence that might deflect or defeat an incoming blow. They became smaller in later periods when fighting on foot was more common than on horseback. Similarly, the *kusazuri* (tassets) provided protection to the groin and upper legs. They were attached to the *dō* by cords and could move independently.

One of the biggest problems when designing body armour is how to put it on, and how to ensure it remains secure. However this is achieved, openings and fastenings can be weak points, so are best located in areas an enemy is unlikely to strike. Many designs of *dō* opened under the right arm, a location less likely to be targeted than the opposite side (assuming a right-handed wearer), since most of a samurai's weapons were wielded from a 'weak side forward' stance.

### NI MAI DŌ ('CLAMSHELL')

The term *ni mai dō,* or 'clamshell', is generally applied to cuirasses that had a hinge at one side, though there were multiple designs. Scale armour with a side opening but no hinge is known as *dō-maru* and appeared in the 11th century. Similar armour with a back opening is *haramaki-dō.* These terms were initially specific but are now used to group armours with similar characteristics, including some from very different time periods.

*A carrying chest for armour, constructed out of leather.*

## Limb protection

Armoured sleeves, or *kote*, protected the arms. Some designs had gauntlets (*tekko*) built in while others left them separate. Construction was relatively light, typically using iron plates or scales fixed to cloth. Although arm protection is important, especially in a situation where slashing swords are a threat, heavy armour will tire the arms quickly and may prevent fast and effective manipulation of a weapon.

Haramaki-do *from the late 18th or early 19th century.*

Excessively heavy arm protection might actually be a liability for a samurai warrior, particularly if the forearms are encumbered or weighed down. The use of *sode* made up for lightness of arm protection, as many blows would land on the shoulder shields rather than arm protection, but the weight of this defence rested mainly on the torso.

For a warrior fighting on foot, the legs were less likely to be hit than the arms, though it was always a possibility. Targeting the legs with a stabbing spear was difficult, though a *naginata* or sword could make an effective cut under the cuirass to strike weakly protected legs. Such a

*The gauntlets and breastplate of this samurai armour are made of stingray skin. Any suitably strong and flexible material could be incorporated in armour, though some were difficult and therefore expensive to obtain.*

stroke is always something of a gamble, however, as the warrior's weapon is lowered out of the path of a counter-stroke at the head or body. However good his armour, a samurai's best defence against such strikes was the threat he projected. An opponent worried about being cloven by an overhead blow might be reluctant to put himself under it.

Lower leg protection was provided by *suneate*, or greaves, which were formed in a similar manner to the kote. Knee protection (*tateage*) became common in later periods, while the foot was protected by *kogake*

*The gauntlets of an Edo period* Nimai Do Gusoku, *or two-piece cuirass armour.*

*Greaves provided lower leg protection, which was important when fighting on horseback or when facing a weapon like the* naginata, *which could make a sweeping low cut.*

made from strips of leather. The upper leg would be protected by the *haidate*, if worn. The *haidate*, or cuisses, appeared relatively late – sometime in the 13th century – and do not seem to have been popular. Although impressive for ceremonial occasions, the *haidate* are said to have been overly encumbering and were generally dispensed with when fighting.

**Under the armour**

What is worn under armour can be as important as the outer layer. Thick padding might offer additional protection against impact or a weapon that has only just managed to penetrate the armour but it is heavy, bulky and hot. Even thinner material can bunch up, restricting movement, or chafe the wearer to the point where wearing armour becomes unbearable.

*The* Haidate, *or skirt, was a form of hanging upper leg protection that offered better freedom of movement than close-fitting armour components.*

Under his armour, an early samurai would wear the traditional *fundoshi* (loincloth or tie) with a shirt (*shitagi*) and belt. Trousers (*hakama*) varied according to the wearer's status; *kobakama* were worn by lower-ranking warriors. The trousers were relatively short, reaching just below the knee. This prevented wet or tangled legwear from restricting the user's movements. Tabi, or slippers, were complemented by *kyahan* – lower-leg coverings tied at the back. Rope sandals called *waraji* went over the tabi to provide grip and to protect the soles of the feet from rough ground. The *kosode*, or short-sleeved coat, completed the outfit.

Although complex, this outfit was practical. Lower legwear and sandals would be worn out far more quickly than other garments, catching on vegetation and stones. They could be easily swapped without

Kobakama *were a subset of the various trouser-like garments (*hakama*) a warrior might wear. They were mostly used by lower-class warriors.*

*Human anatomy is not well suited to being armoured, even without the need to mount and ride a horse while wearing it. The* Haidate, *or skirt, was a potential solution, although many historians doubt it was frequently used.*

throwing away the parts of the garment that were still serviceable. Over time, the clothing of a samurai evolved. The *kosode* was originally of undyed silk, but later it became common to richly decorate it. The kimono replaced the kosode in the Edo period (1603–1868).

The *kosode* or *kimono* was stylish as well as practical. Its tough silk construction resisted the chafing effect of armour and provided a last measure of protection in the event of penetration. Designs have evolved over the years, and while armour has faded out of fashion the clothing worn with it has remained a symbol of all things Japanese.

Clothing worn with and without armour varied over time and from place to place. A two-piece suit known as *kamishino* appeared during the classical period (10th–15th centuries), to be worn over a *kimono*. Leather boots replaced the *tabi* and sandals in later periods, though not all warriors could afford them.

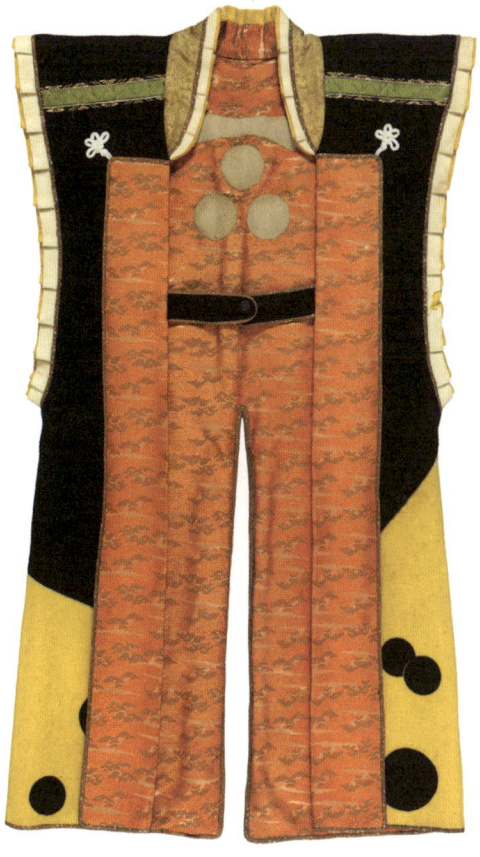

*This beautifully-made early 19th century surcoat contrasts with the traditional straw sandals (warajai) used by samurai. Sandals were disposable yet provided good grip and support for the sole of the foot.*

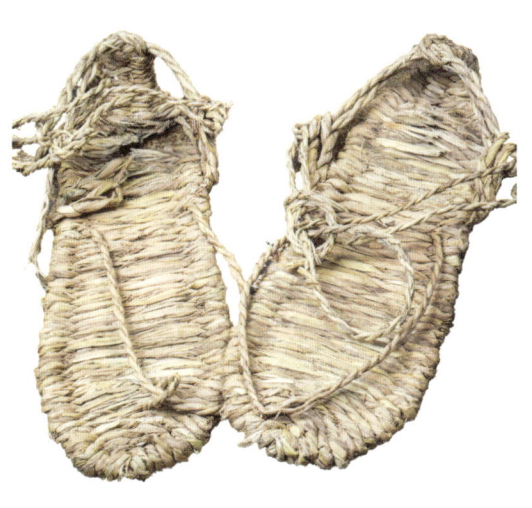

*Simple* hitatare *robes were worn under trousers with draw strings under the knee.*

# DONNING ARMOUR

Putting on anything but the simplest of protective equipment can be a complex task that might require the assistance of one or more servants. In general, samurai armour was donned over clothing, from the legs to the arms and body and finally the head. The greaves were first tied round the lower legs, then the tassets round the waist if they were to be worn.

Gloves and armoured sleeves might be a single piece or separate ones. Once these were in place the samurai put on his cuirass and shoulder shields. The face mask, throat protector and helmet were put on last and taken off first, though there was an adage among samurai that once the battle was over it was wise to tighten the helmet straps. This was in part an admonition not to celebrate too soon and perhaps be dispirited by a sudden change in fortunes, and in part a reference to the need to see the task through to its end. Given the nature of Japanese politics at the time, the aftermath of a battle might be just the beginning of a struggle to make the victory worth something. History is littered with examples of armies that won their war only to throw away their gains at the negotiating table.

Kusazuri were attached to protect the legs, and then kote gauntlets were added. After adding padding to the upper arms armour was hung over the shoulders and secured with a complex system of cords.

*Finally* sode *sleeves were added, along with swords, a* nodowa *to protect the lower face, and then a cloth band (*hachimaki*) was wrapped around the head, and face mask attached before the helmet was worn.*

*Satirical French 19th century print with sequential pictures showing a Japanese Samurai warrior dressing in his robes. Based on Japanese sources.*

**Transport and display**

Perhaps the simplest way to transport a suit of armour would be to wear it, but this is not always practicable. Even the best-made armour becomes uncomfortable and tiring after a while, and wear is inevitable. Chips in the lacquer or worn cords had to be repaired, at the very least costing a considerable sum and possibly taking the armour out of commission when it was needed.

The usual solution was to store armour in a soft cloth bag, inside a protective wooden chest known as a *kara-bitsu* or 'Chinese chest'. This suggests the practice or at least the design of the box came from China or somewhere on the Asian mainland. The box would have had rope handles for carrying by servants if the armour's owner could afford them. If not, it was fitted with straps to be carried on his own back. A lighter chest, called a *gusoku-bitsu*, was also used.

The same chest was used to display armour when not in use. A half-stand constructed of wood stood atop the *kara-bitsu*, with the armour placed upon it. The *kabuto* and any face protection associated with the armour was displayed atop the stand, with the armour below giving the impression that the owner was sitting on the chest.

The karabitsu *(literally, Chinese chest) is a rectangular lidded chest raised on four legs. The name implies a foreign origin for this elegant and functional form, used in Japan since the Nara period (645–794) to store precious objects.*

CHAPTER 4

# Ancient Samurai Armour (4th–9th centuries)

It is likely that the first recognizable samurai armour was developed from designs used on the mainland of Asia. During Japan's long period of isolation, armour design was based solely on internal influences, with new techniques and requirements appearing once contact was resumed with the outside world. Armour in use before the 10th century is classified as ancient.

*Opposite: Tomb figures are used in many cultures to guard the honoured dead. This Japanese warrior figure dates from some time in the fourth to the sixth century.*

*An earthenware representation of a Kofun period (sixth century) Japanese warrior.*

**Tankō**

The earliest samurai armour dates from the fourth century. The version intended for combat on foot was known as *tankō* and consisted of body and head protection. The cuirass was rather difficult to put on, requiring the wearer to pull it open at the front – usually with assistance from others – and lace it shut once inside. Later designs were hinged at the side for easier access. The *tankō* cuirass featured shoulder shields and armour skirts, making it the earliest recognizable samurai armour. Construction was initially laced, though riveted lamellae appeared later.

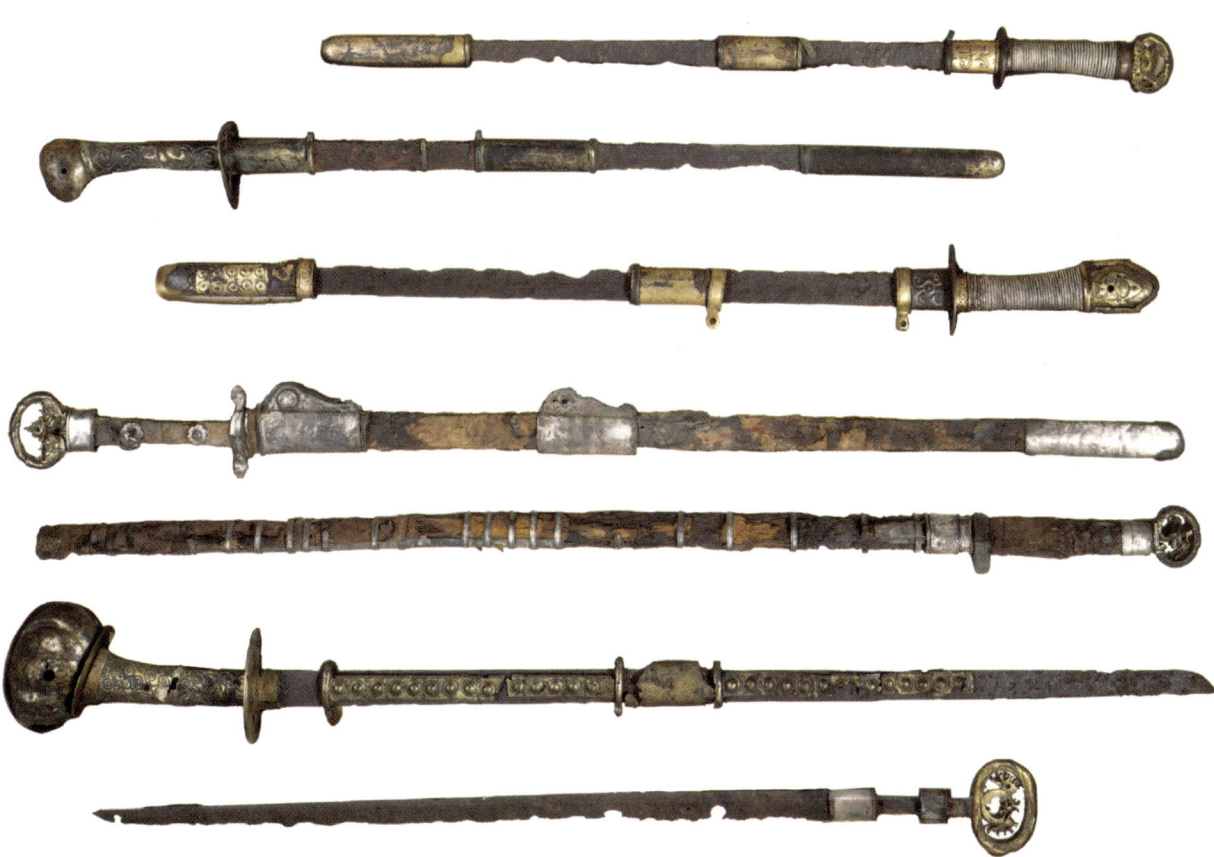

*Straight-bladed Chinese swords dating from the beginning of the seventh century. Weapons such as these heavily influenced early Japanese sword making.*

*While swords are more glamorous, spears such as the straight-bladed* yari *are the arbiters of history – whether in the hands of samurai or common foot soldiers.*

*Constructed of horizontal iron plates, this* tanko *provided good protection against the weaponry of fifth century Japan.*

The battlefield weapon of choice at this time was the *hoko yari*, a straight-bladed spear, which armed common warriors as well as samurai. Although eclipsed by the glamour of the sword, spears penetrate armour better and have a much greater reach. They can also be used when fighting in close order, whereas a long cutting sword requires more space for each warrior. They are also cheap.

*A 19th century depiction of a general ordering the assault force to advance during the 1575 battle of Nagashino Castle.*

*Terra cotta warrior figurine from the Kofun period, intended to be included among grave goods for an important person.*

The *tankō* offered layers of defence against a thrust with such a weapon. Ideally, the shoulder shields would deflect a spear past the warrior or it would slide off the curved surface of the cuirass. A point that was fixed posed a much more serious threat, since the flexion of the spear haft magnified force that was concentrated at the tip.

**Keikō**

The *keikō*, or 'hanging armour', was contemporary with the *tankō*. It was developed to suit the needs of the mounted warrior and was based on Korean designs using scale construction rather than lamellae. The early

*A Kofun period tomb figurine of a warrior in* keiko-*style armour.*

*keikō* was similar to the *tankō*, but by the eighth century a more advanced version had appeared. This consisted of two halves joined by shoulder straps and was easier to don.

When fighting on foot, leg protection is not always essential. A spear-armed opponent could certainly hit the legs but doing so is tricky; a thrust towards the centre of body mass is more likely to strike home. However, on horseback the legs are in a more convenient location to be

*According to legend, the demon Ibaraki-doji tried to ambush the great samurai Watanabe no Tsuna by pretending to be a beautiful woman in distress.*

*This set of armour (Gusoku) was made in the 18th century by Myochin Munesuke, except for the helmet which dates from the 16th century. The latter was made by Saotome Ietada.*

struck and indeed may be the only target an opponent can reach. For this reason, *keikō* armour sometimes included leg protection of similar construction to the cuirass. What was effectively a tube of scales wrapped round the leg and was tied at the rear.

### *DŌ-MARU* ('BODY WRAP')

Exactly when the *dō-maru*, or 'body wrap', appeared is debatable. It was in widespread use during the early part of the classical period and was probably available in some form well before this. *Dō-maru* armour was flexible and lightweight and could be donned more quickly than more elaborate protection. This made it popular for situations where the samurai might need greater mobility or where a sudden threat might present itself.

*Dō-maru* was also relatively inexpensive, so it could be used to armour non-samurai troops and retainers. In the classical period it was used as an alternative to the heavy *ō-yoroi* for situations where the samurai would not be fighting on horseback. It was constructed in a similar manner of other armours, with a chestpiece of lamellae and attached skirts to protect the lower body without interfering with freedom of movement. In place of large shoulder shields, *dō-maru* armour had small plates called *gyoyo*, which provided additional protection but only to the shoulders.

*A 16th century* Dō-maru. *With its green, white, and vermillion lacing, this cuirass is a rare and fine example from that time.*

*Left: Fourteenth century* Sode, *or shoulder guard.*

*Below: The small gap between the extended helmet and the shoulder guards of this 14th century armour made it unlikely an enemy's blow or arrow could slip between to strike the wearer's head.*

**Helmets**

Naturally, head protection evolved alongside armour. The helmet associated with the *tankō* incorporated an early form of the *mabizashi* ('visor-like protrusion'), which became characteristic of Japanese helmets. The generic term for all helmets of this type is *mabizashi-tsuke kabuto*, or

*A 15th century* kabuto *with crest.*

'visor-attached helmet', though this type was referred to as *shokaku-tsuke kabuto* in reference to its resemblance to a warship's ramming prow.

A different helmet was associated with the *keikō*. This was known as *mabizashi-tsuke kabuto* for its visor. The design of these helmets was sophisticated, incorporating a central ridge to increase strength and redirect the force of a blow along with additional neck protection. The design evolved through the ancient period, with some later helmets showing what appear to be Mongolian influences.

Shokakutsuki kabuto, *probably dating from the eighth century.*

*A depiction of the samurai general Sakanoue no Karitamaro (727–786) drawing his bow.*

CHAPTER 5

# *Classical Samurai Armour (10th–15th centuries)*

THE CLASSICAL PERIOD of Japanese armour design begins in the 10th century and ends with the appearance of multiple new types due to outside contact in the 15th century. During this period armour design was based on well-known threats and well-established social norms. At the beginning of this period samurai were primarily mounted archers and were most likely to be threatened by arrows shot by their opposing counterparts.

*Opposite: A mounted archer with his tall bow. Using such a weapon from horseback required years of practice.*

*The female samurai general Tomoe Gozen defeats Uchida Ieyoshi at the 1184 battle of Awazu no Hara.*

Warriors were armed with swords as personal weapons, but it was not until well into the classical period that the sword became the primary weapon of the samurai. The katana, in a recognizable form, emerged during this period as the result of a long evolution that began before the Heinan period with copies of Chinese weapons.

## Ō-yoroi

The *ō-yoroi*, or 'great armour', began to appear in the 10th century and became perhaps the definitive samurai armour. At the time the primary mode of combat for samurai was as horse archers. Their armour had to permit shooting and also protect against arrows. This difficult problem

*Legendary swordsmith Gorō Nyūdō Masamune (c.1264–1343) forges a* katana *blade.*

*Minamoto no Tametomo (1139–1170) was an excellent archer who fought on the losing side of the Hogen Disturbance and was exiled as punishment.*

was solved by creating what amounted to an armoured box around the torso with additional protection for the left side.

Construction used similar methods to other armour types, with the addition of larger iron plates in some areas. These were covered, inside and out, by leather. The size of the *yumi*, the great samurai bow, meant that shooting to the right was impractical even if the warrior's armour permitted it. It was therefore only necessary to be able to aim in a fairly limited arc to the left of the horse's head.

*Sasaki Takatsuna (1160–1214) crosses the river Uji to lead the attack at the 1184 second battle of Uji, during the Genpei War.*

The result of this was that – unless he became surrounded – a samurai would always be facing the same way towards his enemies, so protection could be optimized in that direction. Armour for the left arm, and a large shoulder shield on that side, enhanced survivability while leaving the right arm free to draw the bow.

The *ō-yoroi* was sufficiently expensive that only high-ranking samurai

*This armour was possessed by the Ashikaga clan, which donated it to the Kurama temple near Kyoto. The helmet bowl was made in the early 14th century, with the rest of the armour dating from the late 14th or early 15th century.*

could afford it, and it was geared to a very specific mode of combat. When operating on foot, samurai used different armour – often the rather humbler *dō-maru*. *Ō-yoroi* became less useful as the samurai became swordsmen rather than archers. However, it remained important as a symbol of their status and underwent a revival during the Edo period when ceremony was more important than warfighting ability.

*Refurbished on the orders of Sakai Tadamochi (1723–1775), who had been military governor of Kyoto in the 1750s, the armour's silk lacings were replaced with rawhide in the earlier style.*

*A warrior armoured in* kusari *(chainmail)*.

**Kusari**

Mail armour, known as *kusari*, was used in Japan but did not become as prevalent as it was in Europe. It is likely mail was being produced before the 10th century, and the technology became highly advanced with many variations on the basic linked-rings concept. However, scale and lamellar armours remained far more popular. It is possible this was due to the nature of Japanese warfare, which at the time relied heavily upon exchanges of arrows between mounted samurai.

Mail was primarily used to link armour pieces or to cover weak points between pieces of more rigid armour, though some all-mail armour pieces were produced and mail did provide a cheaper alternative to traditional Japanese armour for non-samurai troops. It was social

*A suit of mail from one of Sandayu Momochi's residences (16th century).*

change that caused a rise in popularity, ironically as the result of a long period of peace.

In the Edo period, wars were few and samurai did not often need protection against spears and arrows. Politics could be rather vigorous, however, and assassination was a real threat. It might not be acceptable to stomp around in full battlefield armour but many samurai considered protection necessary. Silk offered some possibilities in terms of protection and was of course acceptable since it was a luxury clothing item, but many samurai took to wearing mail under their outer clothes.

## CONSTRUCTION METHODS

*Kusari* differed from European mail in terms of its construction and use. It might be sewn between layers of cloth, such as when creating an armoured sleeve, or fixed to a foundation in the manner of scale armour. In this case circular rings were attached to the foundation and linked to oval ones.

Rings were typically butted together rather than being riveted, though after contact with Europeans became more common, riveting increased in popularity. Solid sections of mail could be produced, but some designs were more open. While the gaps this created were obviously more susceptible to impaling attacks such as spears and arrows, protection against cutting weapons was not greatly diminished, creating a worthwhile trade-off in terms of weight.

*Samurai armoured in* kusari katabira, *offering them good protection at the expense of a certain lack of style.*

*Riveting displaced butting as a means of constructing chainmail after contact with Europeans.*

### Hara-ate and haramaki

Another option for concealed wear was the *hara-ate*, or 'armour of the abdomen'. This consisted of a light version of the traditional cuirass that protected only the front of the torso. *Hara-ate* was developed to protect low-ranking foot soldiers such as *ashigaru* but was found useful by samurai desiring discreet protection.

The *hara-ate* did not protect against a knife in the back, which was a real possibility at the time. More comprehensive protection was offered by *haramaki*, which did have a back plate. This was rather unkindly known as a 'coward's plate', as a samurai was supposed to always face his enemies. The introduction of both these armour types resulted from a change in

*Left: An 18th century* hara-ate. *Armour of this sort would protect the vital organs from a stabbing attack and could be worn under clothing.*

*Right: A 15th or 16th century* haramaki, *providing less discreet but more comprehensive protection. The 'coward's plate' at the rear might be more important in a social or political situation than on the battlefield.*

*An armour set from the Kamakura period (1185–1333).*

the way wars were fought. Samurai were no longer primarily horse archers and were more likely to fight on foot with the spear or their swords. At the same time armies were becoming much larger.

Giving common soldiers at least basic protection was a good investment. Not only would their lord benefit from experienced troops who survived their battles, but armour also improved morale. Even a little protection is reassuring when the enemy is advancing, so troops were less likely to rout if they had some armour.

*Nasu no Yoichi (c1169–c1232) was renowned for his prowess as an archer. He is said to have shot a fan off the mast of a vessel from a moving horse – on his first attempt.*

**Head and face protection**

Where early samurai armour protected only the head and torso, additional items became common in the classical era. The face mask and throat protector began to become prevalent in the 11th century and gradually became standard for all samurai armour.

The throat protector, or gorget, can be generically referred to as *nodawa*. Various terms existed for specifics, such as how the gorget fastened. Once the face mask (*menpo* or *men yoroi*) became standard it was usually integrated with the gorget and became known as *yodare-kake*. Essentially, the *yodare-kake* was now a component of the *menpo* rather than being a piece of armour in its own right.

Specific terms refer to the different ways of providing face protection, with or without an integral gorget. The term *menpo* is often

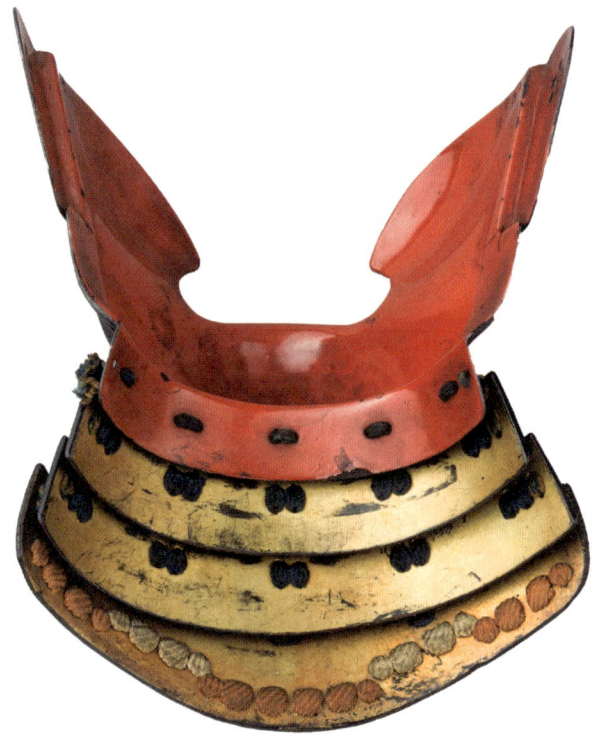

*Various designs of face mask existed, some with integral throat protection and some requiring it to be worn separately. The overlapping plates allowed the wearer to tilt his head up and down.*

*A full face mask (somen) with integral throat protection.*

loosely applied to all face protection, through correctly it applies to a half-mask covering the face from the eyeline down. A full mask is termed shomen. Both have the capability to be highly decorated in a generally fearsome manner, with demonic features, huge moustaches and terrifying expressions.

The hanbo combined a mask for the lower face and chin with throat protection formed from multiple overlapping lamellae. These provided effective protection but still allowed the wearer to move his head freely and to tuck in his chin. The latter might be important when facing a downward blow. By hunching up, the samurai could take the impact on

*A separate throat protector, or* nodowa, *dating from the late 18th or early 19th century.*

*Face masks were not merely functional. These examples from the 18th century were made in a ferocious and decorative style by the Myochin clan.*

his *kabuto*, hoping its shape would deflect most of the force and that its mabizashi would guide the weapon past his face. Rigid neck protection would not permit such a movement and might actually be a liability in this situation.

Similar to the *hanbo*, the *hoate* protected the chin, cheeks and lower half of the face, again with a gorget of overlapping lamellae. While not as protective as a full mask, armour of this sort offered unimpeded breathing and vision.

The *happuri*, or open-face armour, was used by *ashigaru* and some low-status samurai to provide at least a measure of protection to the forehead and cheeks. It was effective against attacks coming in anywhere apart from directly into the wearer's face, meaning that an instinctive last-second duck or flinch could save the wearer. Vision and breathing were not impaired.

*Mid-14th century* kabuto. *Although there was some standardisation of technique and design, helmet construction varied considerably.*

**Evolving kabuto design**

At the beginning of the classical period helmets tended to be complex and time-consuming to construct. This was entirely acceptable since they were used only by a relatively small number of well-off warriors. Increasing use of *ashigaru*, and a desire to give them some protection, necessitated a simple helmet design.

The standard samurai helmet might have 24 or more plates making up its dome. Some had over a hundred. Simpler helmets with fewer plates – as few as six in some cases – and a more basic design became common for poor samurai and *ashigaru*. The latter were often equipped with a *jingasa*, or 'war hat', which might be made up of one or several iron plates. Designs varied, with some being nothing more than a skullcap.

After Portuguese traders began to arrive in the mid-1500s, a variety of helmets collectively called *namban-kabuto* – essentially 'helmets of the southern barbarians' – began to emerge. These included foreign helmets modified to suit Japanese preference as well as local designs influenced by them.

*A* kabuto *from the Nanbokucho period (1336–92) with a prominent crest to identify the user's status and allegiance.*

*A* zunari kabuto *dating from the Edo period.*

Another style that emerged during this period became known as *zunari-kabuto*, translating as 'head-shaped helmet'. The *kawari-kabuto*, or 'exotic helmet', usually had a *zunari-kabuto* as its base, augmented with sometimes bizarre decoration formed from leather, wood and other lightweight materials.

*The relative simplicity of the* zunari kabuto *is used as the base for this elaborately decorated* kawari kabuto *dating from the 19th century. The base helmet itself may be older than the crest.*

CHAPTER 6

# Modern Samurai Armour (16th–19th centuries)

TOSEI-GUSOKU, or modern armour, appeared in the 16th century, using new techniques and concepts learned from outsiders and in response to the appearance of early firearms. Some experimental or transition types incorporated traditional elements as well as new ones, creating a wide variety of armours that can only be generally grouped by characteristics or construction methods.

*Opposite: Koboto Santoro, a senior military commander, pictured in 1868 wearing traditional armour and carrying the signature weapons of the samurai warrior.*

*Helmet accompanying* mogami-do *style armour, dating from the 17th or 18th century.*

## Mogami-dō

Possibly named for the Mogami region, this type of chest armour used five large plates rather than tightly overlapping scales. These were laced using a technique called *sugake odoshi*, which was far less dense than the usual *kebiki odoshi* technique.

It was relatively light and simple to manufacture due to less dense lacing than more traditional armours. Side-opening and back-opening variants were produced, making mogami-dō a general type identified by construction method. Mogami-type chest armour appeared in the Muromachi period (1336–1573), though it was uncommon, and was used as a component of later, 'modern', armour types.

*Left & below: Horizontal metal plates became a common construction method in the 'modern' period of samurai armour-making. At the same time the details of construction, such as number of plates and their relative size, began to vary considerably.*

## Maru-dō

The use of lamellar construction was not common in the classical period of samurai armour-making but became more popular in later years. There was still a need for relatively light armour for foot combat, causing the *dō-maru* concept to be revisited. *Maru-dō* was similar in most ways, with the opening under the right arm, but was constructed of lamellae rather than scales.

*The use of large lamellae (plates) rather than scales had advantages over scale construction. Not only was the armour easier and quicker to make but protection against piercing weapons, such as bullets, was improved.*

*This armour of the* morohada-nugi-dō gusoku *type uses an unusual cuirass design intended to mimic a bare human torso. It was produced some time in the 17th century.*

### OKEGAWA-DŌ

Often translated as 'tub-sided' armour, *okegawa-dō* appeared in the mid-16th century. It used riveted rather than laced lamellae. The movement away from lacing was characteristic of modern armours, enabling armour to be produced more quickly and easily, though it was not universal.

*After the appearance of the* namban, *or 'southern barbarians' in Japan, armour and helmet design began to show European influences. This helmet is reminiscent of the felt hats worn by the early Portuguese traders.*

**Namban-dō**

The 'armour of the southern barbarians' takes its name from a reference to the Portuguese mariners who first arrived in Japan in 1543. They possessed matchlock firearms, which, while primitive by modern standards, were an unpleasant surprise for the Japanese. Traditional armour was not effective against these weapons so naturally Japanese armour-makers chose to copy the armour of those who had experience facing them.

Japanese armour was uniquely suited to swapping out components, and in this case the traditional cuirass was replaced by a single-piece plate chest protector of distinctly European style. Armour of this sort was too expensive for most samurai.

*Both images: The first photographs of samurai were taken in the 1860s. This image depicts a samurai holding a jousting pole.*

*A photograph taken by Felice Beato (1832–1909) depicting a samurai armed with an asymmetric bow.*

## Variants

During this period a great many variants emerged, in some cases based on a mix of scale and lamellae construction or incorporating single plates and larger sections of mail than had previously been common in Japanese

*Japanese armour was eminently suited to replacement of parts and reuse of others. Some armour components date from the Edo period, with a* kabuto *in the Edo style but of later construction.*

armour-making. Examples include suits of armour where the cuirass is of scale construction and other pieces used lamellae, or armour constructed in the traditional manner except for the armoured sleeves, which were of European-influenced design. Various terms have been coined for these hybrid pieces, some specific to a single combination of construction methods and some used more generally.

*Mid 19th century armour. By this time Western nations had all but abandoned the use of personal armour due to the difficulty of making protection both effective against the weapons of the day and light enough to move in.*

*A* kabuto *(helmet) and* menpo *(face mask), late Edo period. The* kabuto *is constructed of 14 plates in the style of an* Akoda Nari *helmet.*

CHAPTER 7

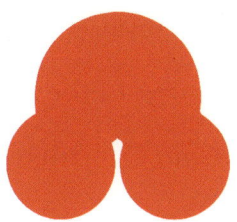

# Famous Samurai of the Sengoku Period

The Sengoku period (1467–1615) produced the definitive, or at least most widely recognized, image of the samurai warrior and the surrounding political landscape. With the shogun as de facto ruler still required to at least pay lip service to the weak emperor, politics were complex at the best of times. Ambitious *daimyo* sought to expand their territory or even bring all of Japan under their control. The most prominent of these laid the foundations for the relatively peaceful Edo period and ultimately modern Japan.

*Opposite: Screen depicting the Battle of Sekigahara, celebrating Tokugawa Ieyasu's victory over Ishida Mitsunari and his supporters. This 1854 replica recreates the original* Hikone-jō Bon Sekigahara Kassen Byōbu *by Sadanobu Kanō from the 1620s and was a treasure of the Lord Ii.*

**Takeda Shingen (1521–73)**

Takeda Shingen was a military innovator of the Sengoku period. His father was Takeda Nobutora, *daimyo* of the Takeda clan whose territory lay on the Kantō Plain in Honshu. Control over this fertile lowland was desired by several clans, leading to an endless cycle of shifting alliances and conflicts.

By 1541, Takeda Nobutora was becoming increasingly unpopular with both his subjects and his retainers. Heavy taxation to support his wars was combined with disaffection within his household, leading to his son Harunobu – the future Shingen – staging a palace revolution. This is generally referred to as a 'bloodless coup', which took place while Takeda Nobutora was away from his stronghold. Takeda Nobutora went

*Despite being ordained as a Buddhist priest, Takeda Shingen was an ambitious warrior who took his clan to the pinnacle of its power during a turbulent era of history.*

*A woodblock print by Utagawa Kunitoshi (1798–1861) of Takeda Shingen.*

into exile, leaving his son at the head of a clan who were, by all accounts, pleased to be rid of him.

The ambitious Takeda Harunobu embarked upon a series of campaigns to expand his territory. Although he became a Buddhist priest in 1551, at which point he took the name Shingen, his martial ambitions did not waver. This brought the Takeda clan once more into conflict with the Uesugi, who were at the time in something of an eclipse. This conflict is the subject of a great many stories, dramas and legends centring on a series of battles between Takeda Shingen and Uesugi Kenshin.

Since 1439 the *daimyo* of the Uesugi clan had held the post of governor-general of the Kantō region, but in 1552 the current *daimyo*, Uesugi Norimasa, was defeated by the Hōjō clan. He fled to Echigo Province, where he found shelter with the Nagao clan. Uesugi Norimasa brought with him the allegiance of many of his vassals, creating a powerful alliance that could challenge the Takeda.

*In 1541 Nobutora Takeda,* daimyo *of Kai province, was deposed by his son, who led the Takeda clan as Takeda Shingen.*

*The battle of Mikatagahara pitted the Takeda clan against the Tokugawa and Oda clans. Tokugawa arquebusiers failed to repel the Takeda cavalry charge, after which the Tokugawa-Oda army was all but destroyed.*

From this merging of clans emerged a warrior, born Nagao Kagetora, but better known to history as Uesugi Kenshin. Having inherited leadership of the Uesugi clan he led them in a series of campaigns known collectively as the 'battles of Kawanakajima'. The first brought armies under Uesugi Kenshin and Takeda Shingen into contact on Kawanakajima Plain in 1553. Initially, the opposing commanders were cautious and did not engage on these occasions, but later in the year as the Takeda clan were withdrawing Shingen attacked and inflicted a defeat.

In 1555, a similarly inconclusive campaign saw Takeda forces under Shingen camped within sight of their enemies for months before political factors caused the campaign to be abandoned. However, in 1557 Shingen

*Uesugi Kenshin was a military genius and an excellent administrator. As a follower of the war-god Bishamonten he epitomised the warrior-ruler.*

made a bold foray into Uesugi territory, capturing one stronghold and threatening another. A countermove by the Uesugi clan resulted in withdrawal.

After years of manoeuvring and threats, the Uesugi clan marched on Kaizu Castle and arrived before it, catching the Takeda clan by surprise. Shingen reacted to this threat with a risky hammer-and-anvil gambit, sending a portion of his force to attack the Uesugi rear. This would, he hoped, drive his opponents on to his main force, which was deployed in a 'crane's wing' formation.

This did not quite go according to plan. While Shingen had used the cover of night to set up his hammer-and-anvil formation, the Uesugi army had also secretly redeployed. Scattering Shingen's screen of arquebusiers and archers, the Uesugi army charged into his formation in a complex manoeuvre known as the 'winding wheel', which was designed to allow units to hit hard, then pull back to rest.

Accounts of the battle speak of an iconic moment when Uesugi Kenshin himself broke through Shingen's headquarters guard and attacked him vigorously. It is said that Shingen had only a war fan to fight with but was able to stop seven sword cuts with it. His armour protected him from three more before Kenshin was driven off by Shingen's guards.

*Yamamoto Kansuke (c.1501–1561) was a talented general in the service of Takeda Shingen. At the fourth battle of Kawanakajima he chose a glorious death in battle over the defeat he believed was imminent.*

The battle turned when Shingen's detached force attacked the Uesugi rear, finally bringing about the hammer-and-anvil action he had planned. The Uesugi clan were ground down and began to retreat, though Shingen could not exploit the opportunity because his force was exhausted. A final encounter in 1564 saw only intermittent skirmishing before both armies withdrew.

This conflict took place at a time when Japanese warfare was in flux. The matchlock musket enabled troops with very little training to pose a threat to veteran samurai, and armies were becoming much larger. Rather than small groups of mounted samurai dominating the battlefield with their bows, large blocks of lightly armoured foot soldiers screened by missile troops were often the arbiters of battle. Takeda Shingen moved his samurai to a different role, arming them with spears to create a force of lancers capable of acting as shock troops.

*Oda Nobunaga (1534–1582) was one of the first to truly appreciate what firearms could achieve on the battlefield, though he met his end through old-fashioned treachery.*

**Oda Nobunaga (1534–82)**

Oda Nobunaga is known to history as 'the great unifier'. He came from a relatively minor samurai clan based in Owari Province on Honshu, inheriting his father's position as *daimyo* in 1551. At this time firearms were being imported into Japan but their importance was not yet realized by most *daimyo*. Oda Nobunaga was the first to appreciate what massed guns could do.

*Oda Nobunaga sought to unify all Japan, and succeeded in bringing about half of it under his control. This was a remarkable achievement in such a turbulent time, requiring meticulous planning and a methodical long-term strategy.*

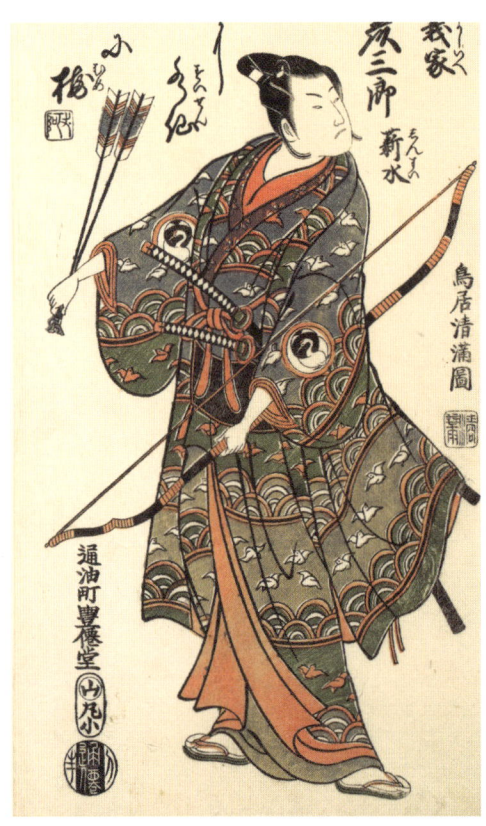

*Appearance was as important to the samurai as their swords, bow or spear.*

Early firearms, even relatively sophisticated ones such as flintlock muskets and rifles, were arguably less effective than bows. Compared to the traditional *yumi*, a matchlock arquebus was a primitive and unreliable thing. It was prone to fouling and might not fire at all if the weather was damp. The *yumi*, on the other hand, had a longer effective range and was more accurate in the hands of a skilled user.

It was that factor – the skill of the user – that was the matchlock's unique advantage. Training an arquebusier to shoot passably well did not take long, especially when all the evolutions of shooting were to be carried out as a drill under close supervision. A volley of musket balls might be random but it was sufficient to pepper an opposing block of infantry and could bring down the noblest warrior if he was unlucky enough to be hit.

Oda Nobunaga was able to see the potential of these weapons andset about ensuring he had enough of them to be decisive. This meant not just buying guns from overseas but creating an arms industry around them. Shot-casting and gunpowder making, as well as construction of the firearms themselves, were essential to his ambitions.

Firepower – especially sustained firepower – can win battles but without strategic direction victories are meaningless. Oda Nobunaga was more than a tactical commander: he had a strategy for long-term conquest. This began with the agricultural resources of the Owari Plain, which were brought entirely under his control by 1560.

Conquest of the Owari region pitted Oda Nobunaga against relatives and other branches of his own clan in the sort of dynastic struggle not uncommon at the time. He immediately faced an external

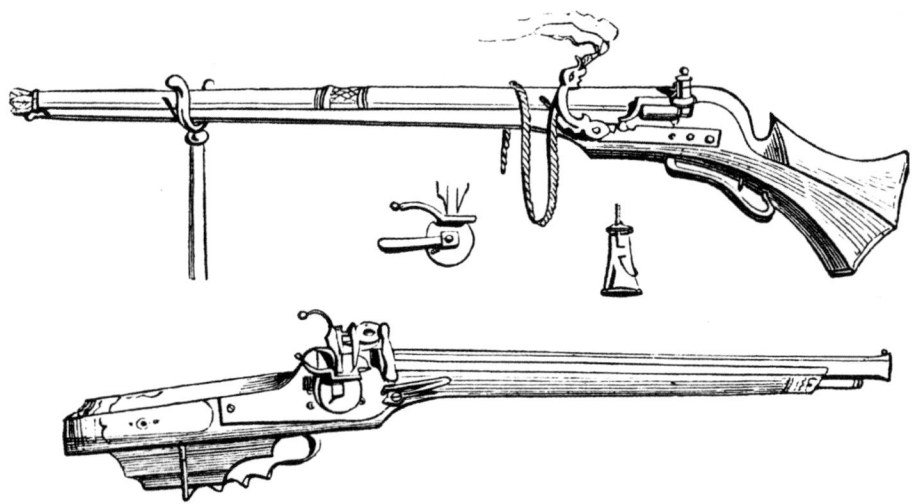

*Matchlock (top) and wheellock (bottom) muskets were crude, unreliable smoothbore weapons that could nevertheless bring down the noblest samurai, and as such were treated with grave suspicion by many.*

threat from forces under the command of Imagawa Yoshimoto. Along with his allies, Yoshimoto had opposed Oda Nobunaga's rise to power and in 1560 he set out to end it once and for all. In addition to his own troops Imagawa Yoshimoto led forces from the Hōjō and Takeda clans. Exact numbers are open to speculation: sources state anything from 20,000 to 40,000 warriors. It is also said that Imagawa Yoshimoto deliberately exaggerated the numbers he commanded to intimidate his opponent.

The campaign was initially successful, capturing Oda fortresses and forcing Oda Nobunaga to take to the field to oppose the advance. Legend has distorted the facts, but it is clear that Oda was heavily outnumbered. He was sufficiently wise to realize that he had to perform a feat of arms or be crushed; a defensive campaign or protracted manoeuvring was a road to ruin. Instead, he resolved to attack vigorously and hope the enemy was too stunned to realize how few they faced.

*For all the size of the forces involved, the battles of Okehazama were greatly influenced by a personal combat between Imagawa Yoshimoto and two Oda samurai who attacked his command post.*

*Oda Nobunaga's victory at Okehazama was due to a grim appraisal of the bad situation he was in and a courageous gamble on an attack against a superior force.*

The decisive clash took place at the village of Okehazama, close to modern Nagoya. The invading army was celebrating its victories and was complacent, allowing Oda Nobunaga's relatively tiny force to get close enough to attack. Imagawa Yoshimoto was killed by two Oda samurai who attacked his headquarters. For all that massed formations were gaining importance, this was an age of heroic leadership, and with their leader dead the invading army routed.

Oda Nobunaga's approach was methodical, securing and pacifying one area before moving on to his next campaign. His obvious talent made it preferable for other *daimyo* to align with him than to fight him, and by 1568 he was what in Europe might have been called a kingmaker. Intervening in a dispute over succession to the shogunate, he installed Ashikaga Yoshiaki, only to depose him in 1573 when he no longer suited Oda's plans.

*At the battle of Nagashino in 1575, Oda Nobunaga used hastily erected palisades to break up the charge of the famed Takeda cavalry, enabling his arquebusiers to dominate the battlefield.*

Oda Nobunaga now more or less controlled Japan. He began a series of economic reforms intended to reduce the sources of income of the *daimyo* and to strengthen his own position. His main opposition was the Ikkō sect, which resisted his attempts to take control of some areas by creating local defensive leagues. It is notable that while a certain courtesy and generosity was expected in dealing with defeated *daimyo*, Oda Nobunaga was not usually merciful towards these bands of peasants and impoverished samurai.

Control was cemented by rewarding those who showed loyalty to the new regime, with land taken from those defeated by it. This was not entirely successful: in 1582 Akechi Mitsuhide – who owed direct loyalty to Oda Nobunaga – betrayed him. Wounded and trapped, Oda committed seppuku. Although it ended in personal defeat, Oda Nobunaga's bid to unify Japan brought about half of it under central control and paved the way for future unification.

*Betrayed by his vassal Akechi Mitsuhide, Oda Nobunaga was besieged in the fortified temple of Honno-ji with a small force of warriors. He denied his enemies total victory by committing* seppuku *and having his body hidden in the burned temple.*

*Statue of Tokugawa Ieyasu, who rebuilt the fortunes of his troubled clan by way of an alliance with Oda Nobunaga, and eventually became unifier of Japan.*

## Tokugawa Ieyasu (1543–1616)

Tokugawa Ieyasu rose from relatively humble origins to become shogun of Japan. His father was Matsudaira Hirotada, who as a minor noble was caught up in the complex politics of the time with little control over his fate. One consequence of this was that in 1547 Tokugawa Ieyasu was sent

*This depiction of Tokugawa Ieyasu emphasises wise governance rather than military power, though in reality both were necessary in founding and maintaining the new shogunate.*

to the Imagawa clan as a hostage but was instead captured by the Oda clan, who held him for two years.

Many cultures worldwide practised a hostage system, whereby the children of nobles would be raised and educated at the court of another clan or family. There, they served partly as collateral against an uprising or betrayal, but at the same time long-term alliances could be forged. Hostages would, if their families complied, be well treated and given all the comforts and benefits of their station. If the political winds blew fair, the hostage-holders were educating and training their next generation of allies.

Thus it was that the young Tokugawa Ieyasu was trained in the arts of war and politics, rising to lead the army of the Imagawa clan. In the interim his own father was killed and the clan had collapsed into infighting. When the head of the Imagawa clan, Yoshimoto, was killed in battle against the forces of Oda Nobunaga, Tokugawa Ieyasu returned to his family estate and began putting affairs in order.

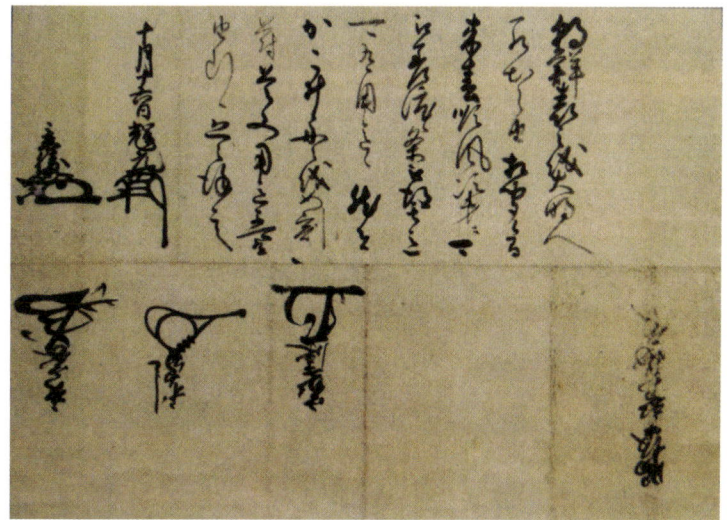

*Above: The joint letter of Toyotomi's Council of Five Elders (go-tairō). In 1598, Toyotomi Hideyoshi formed the Council of Five Elders. The council was designed to protect Hideyoshi's interests and legacy upon his death. Tokugawa Ieyasu was one of the elders, and eventually emerged as shogun.*

*Left: Owned by Ishida Mitsunari (1559–1600), this armour features an extensive crest and a mane of wild hair intended to give the wearer an intimidating, demonic appearance.*

*Opposite: In 1563, Ikko-ikki rebels took up arms against samurai rule, prompting Tokugawa Ieyasu to march against them. Although his armour was repeatedly pierced by bullets, Tokugawa Ieyasu was not injured. He heroic example caused many rebel samurai to return their allegiance to the shogunate.*

*In 1582 the defeated forces of the Takeda clan were cornered by Oda Nobunaga, bringing about a final act of defiance known as the battle of Tenmokuzan. Forty-one samurai under Takeda Katsuyori (1546–1582) executed their families then launched a suicidal charge at their enemies.*

By cultivating an alliance with Oda Nobunaga, Tokugawa Ieyasu was able to secure his lands and deal with minor rebellions without getting involved in large-scale conflict. As the Imagawa clan collapsed, he expanded his territory and launched programmes to improve stability and economic well-being. In an era of conflict and turbulence, stability was a precious commodity, and Tokugawa Ieyasu's domain benefited greatly. This period of growth was threatened when Oda Nobunaga was betrayed.

Tokugawa Ieyasu found himself at odds with Toyotomi Hideyoshi, Oda's successor, but after some skirmishing he was able to obtain favourable terms. Essentially, having assured Hideyoshi he was not a

*The 1600 Battle of Sekigahara brought the Sengoku period to an end and established the Tokugawa shogunate. The severed heads of 40,000 enemy warriors were displayed to Tokugawa Ieyasu after the battle.*

*Kimura Shigenari (1593–1615) led forces of the Toyotomi clan at the siege of Osaka Castle. He led a bold attack on the besieging shogunate forces and was killed on the field of battle. Tokugawa Ieyasu is depicted here examining his severed head after the battle.*

threat, Tokugawa Ieyasu was free to govern his own territory without interference. He did, though, assist in the subjugation of the Hōjō clan, receiving their territory in return for giving up some of his own to create a natural frontier.

Tokugawa Ieyasu was wise enough to stay out of Hideyoshi's attempt to build an overseas empire. Hideyoshi had ambitions in Korea and the Philippines but met disaster in two mainland expeditions, which ended overseas involvement for centuries. In the meantime Tokugawa Ieyasu set up a new capital near Edo and began rationalizing land ownership. His most powerful vassals were given positions of honour along the borders, where they would be kept busy dealing with troublesome outsiders.

In 1598 Hideyoshi formed the Council of Five Elders, powerful lords to whom he entrusted his realm as regents for his young son. He died shortly afterwards, leaving Tokugawa Ieyasu in a position to take control. His forces were large and well organized, and after a period of resistance the other four regents were decisively defeated.

Tokugawa Ieyasu was appointed as shogun by the emperor in 1603. He strengthened his hold on Japan by implementing a large-scale version of the hostage system. Each *daimyo* had to maintain a suitable – that is, lavish to the point of excess – residence at Edo, and even when the *daimyo* returned to his own lands his family had to stay there. In this manner Tokugawa Ieyasu drained funds from the *daimyo* who might oppose him but also held their families where he could control them.

### STABILITY

It was during the Edo shogunate that the class system was formalized and entry to the samurai class closed. Other reforms included disarmament of the peasant class, with restrictions on anything that could be used as a weapon. Tokugawa Ieyasu had brought to an end the period of Warring States and ushered in an era of peace and isolationism that would see the samurai trying to redefine themselves as paragons of virtue who were also warriors.

CHAPTER 8

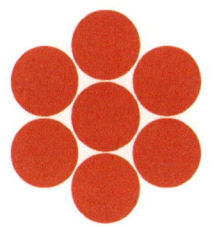

# *Heraldry*

The symbols, or *mon*, used by Japanese noble houses were less closely regulated than those in Europe but served a similar purpose. Likewise, the patterns and symbols used on banners and ceremonial items helped identify notable individuals and their supporters from a distance. This was obviously important on the battlefield, to prevent clashes between friendly troops, but also had important political and social implications.

*Opposite: This 18th century armour displays the plum blossom emblem of the Maeda clan, who ruled Kaga province.*

Status, and due respect shown to status, was extremely important in Japanese society. Being able to tell who the band of samurai guards approaching along a dusty road were protecting might be as vital to political well-being as to survival in the short term. Knowing this was not a hostile force would influence tactical considerations but receiving their lord with courtesy appropriate to his rank and current relations helped avoid other problems.

A noble who showed too much deference to a less powerful lord might seem weak, undermining his status with his own supporters and perhaps making negotiations more complex by starting from a position of perceived weakness. On the other hand, failing to show appropriate respect might anger a superior or someone the noble hoped to influence. A little warning about who was approaching would allow time for preparations to be made.

*The sheath for this spearhead bears the* mon *of the Matsudaira clan, a branch of the Minamoto family.*

*Opposite: Takamatsu Castle, owned by the Mori clan, was besieged in 1582 by forces loyal to Oda Nobunaga. After unsuccessful attacks, Oda Nobunaga ordered the construction of an embankment which caused the coastal castle to be flooded.*

*A woodblock print by Toyohara Chikanobu (1838–1921) depicting the Empress visiting the Third National Industrial Promotional Exhibition in 1890.*

Certain symbols were reserved for the use of the imperial family and household. While there was no college of heraldry to oversee and assign the use of symbols, someone who adopted a reserved motif could be seen as challenging or insulting the emperor. Even if there was no direct response, an act of this sort could be used as a pretext by a potential enemy. However, some noble houses were permitted to use reserved symbols as part of their heraldry as a reward for service.

**The kiku and other mon**

The imperial family adopted the *kiku*, a chrysanthemum with 16 petals, as its symbol. This was probably during the 700s CE. At first a preferred association, the relationship between the chrysanthemum and the imperial household was gradually formalized, with branches of the family using a chrysanthemum with a different number of petals as their emblems. Representing long life, the chrysanthemum has remained the imperial emblem ever since. At the time of the Meiji Restoration (1868–9) a decree was passed that no *mon* that could be mistaken for the imperial symbol could be used.

The first directory of *mon* was published in the early 1500s, but it is not clear when the use of heraldic symbols became widespread. It is likely that adoption was gradual and began centuries earlier. It is known that in the 11th century members of the imperial court displayed *mon* on their clothing, and when the warrior class was ennobled to become recognizable as samurai they adopted family crests – known as *kamon* – to identify themselves.

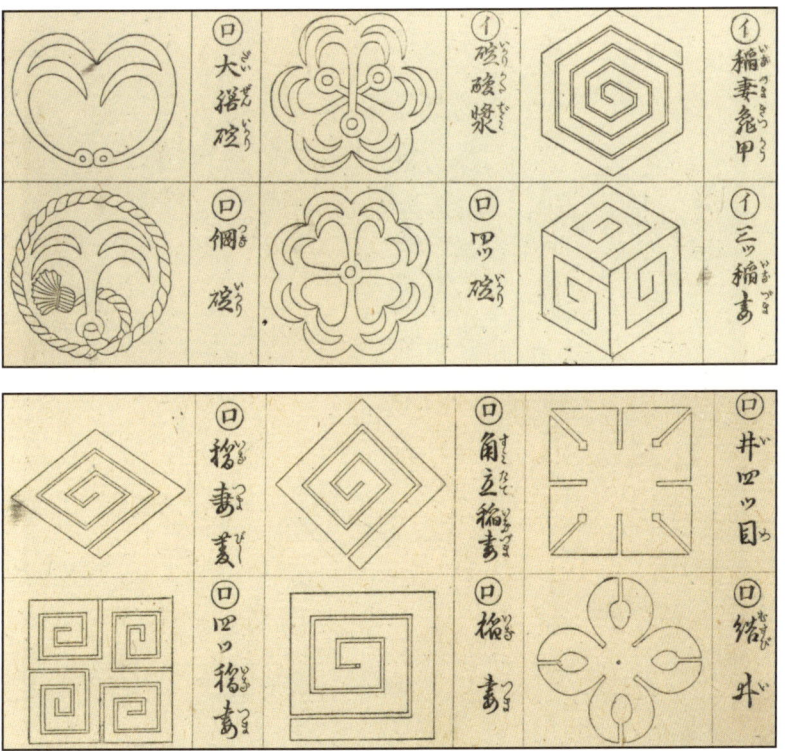

*A catalogue of* mon, *dating from 1881.*

*Samurai armour bearing the emblem of the Minamoto clan.*

Use of crests spread beyond the samurai class, particularly after the end of the turbulent Sengoku period. The harsh necessity of identifying friends and foes on the battlefield was greatly diminished, but *mon* were commercially useful for brand identity, demonstrating membership of an association or to give non-nobles a feeling of increased respectability.

*Mon* incorporate a variety of designs, which can be divided into broad categories. From the natural world there are plants, animals and inanimate natural objects, with shapes and characters, abstract designs and depictions of artificial objects coming from the human mind. A *mon* might be enclosed, though there were no hard-and-fast rules about shapes and colour/metal combinations like those found in European heraldry.

### *Mon* on war banners

*Mon* were also displayed on the *sashimono,* or war banner. Those carried by individuals were originally known as *hata-jirushi,* or symbol-flags. They were simple banners designed to stream in the wind and were square or rectangular in shape. The smallest of these might be attached to a pole worn on the back of a samurai or *ashigaru,* bearing the *mon* of the soldier's lord and possibly additional insignia to help identify formations. A larger version was worn by a unit leader.

Traditionally, the *sashimono* was blank on one side and displayed the clan emblem on the other. Some particularly notable samurai wore their own *mon* to identify themselves to friend and foe alike. There are parallels with European shield and banner emblems and with the distinctively painted fighter aircraft of World War I. In addition to striking fear into enemies, a personal *mon* ensured everyone knew who was performing the great exploits unfolding in front of them.

*Warriors and commanders displaying their banners during the battles of Kawanakajima (1553–1564).*

The practice of displaying a banner became more prevalent in the latter half of the Sengoku period (1467–1615), as warfare became more or less constant and forces much larger. At this time, the *hata-jirushi* was

Mon *would be prominently displayed on the* Jinbaori, *or surcoat, to indicate identity or allegiance. Depicted here are the three oak leaves in a circle of the Makino clan (right) and the* mon *of the Ito clan (below).*

partially replaced by the *nobori*, which was stiffened to be more visible in calm conditions. Typically, banners were used to denote subdivisions or units within an army and were by definition distinctive. However, some commanders chose to display a host of identical banners as a means to intimidate enemies with an impression of a vast host. The largest of these flags, known as *nagarebata* or floating banners, were held aloft by a team of flag-bearers or displayed on static mounts to identify rallying points and command positions.

## MODERN *MON*

From its beginnings as a means of identifying warriors on the battlefield, Japanese heraldry has become a political and commercial tool and remains in use today. A clan emblem might become the symbol of a company, or new *mon* may be created to identify a shop, restaurant or private business. The use of a *mon* in this way is a statement that the owner is not afraid to let everyone know who they are. In effect, displaying a *mon* means the owner has chosen not to hide in anonymity and must stand by their deeds. This can be taken as a promise to behave honourably and to answer for any failures. In that, the role of the *mon* has not really changed since the days of the Warring States.

# Index

Page references in **bold** indicate an illustration.

Abe clan 35
*Akazone* armour **84**
Akechi Mitsuhide 200
arm protection 119–21
armour-making, development 74–88
*ashigaru* 51–6, 162, 169
Ashikaga clan 57
Ashikaga Takauji 45–7, **49**, **105**
Ashikaga Yoshiaki 199
Ashikaga Yoshiteru 58
Asuka period (538–710) 28
Azuchi-Momoyana period (1603–1868) 58–70

banners 90, 211, 217–21
belts 125
boots 126
bows 14, **16**, 77, **95**, 149, 150, **154**, 155, **165**, **182**
breastplates
    ancient Japan **75**, 78
    design and development 111–18
    *hara-ate* and *haramaki* 162
    modern period 176–84
    'proving' marks 81
    stingray skin **121**
    Western influences **71**, 83
Buddhism, arrival in Japan 28
*bushi* 8
*bushidō* 8, *41*, 88

chainmail **158**, 159–60, **161**, **162**
chests (storage and transport) **119**, 132–3
Christianity 57
chrysanthemum *kiku* 214–15
clamshell cuirasses 118
class system 9–12, 25, 61, 209
coats 125, 126
construction of armour
    chainmail 160
    lamellae and scales 92, 94–6
    plate 92, 176, **185**
    *tatami dō 113*, **116**
cords 102
cost of armour 17, 20, 156–7
Council of Five Elders **205**, 209
crests 110, **111**, 215–17
cuirasses **75**, 111–18, 137

*daimyo* 10, 51, 209
*daishō 13*, **16**
Dannoura, Battle of 38, **39**
*datemono* 110
displaying armour 133
*dō 111–18 see also* breastplates; cuirasses
*dō-maru* **85**, 118, 144, **145**, 157, 178
donning armour **128**, **129**, **130-2**

Edo period (1603–1868) 58–70
emperors *see* Imperial power

face masks 105, 108–9, **110**, 131, 166–9
fastening locations 118
feudalism 31, 33
fighting techniques 20, 41, 121–2
firearms 57, 80–1, 83, 181, 194, 195–7
foot protection 121–2
Former Nine Years' War 35
Fujiwara clan 31
*fundoshi* 125
furnaces 76

gauntlets 119, **121**, **122**, 130
Genkō War **13**, 45
Genpei War **15**, 38, **155**
Go-Daigo (Takaharu) 44–7
gorget 166
greaves 122–3
gunpowder 80
guns 57, 80–1, 83, 181, 194, 195–7
*gusoku-bitsu* 133
*gyoyo* 144

*hachimaki* **131**
*haidate* 123, **124**, 126
*hakama* 125
*hanbo* 168
*happuri* 169
*hara-ate* 162, **163**
*haramaki-dō* *96*, **117**, *120*, *162*–5
*hata-jirushi* 217, 218
*hei-no-rokugu* 104
Heian period (794–1185) 30–8
Heiji Disturbance **10**, 36
helmets
    ancient Japan 27, **78**, 147–8
    classical period 170–2, **173**
    design and development 105–10
    donning **131**
    Edo period (1603–1868) 64
    modern period **176**, **185**
    Western influences 171, **180**

helms 108–9
heraldry **210**, 211–21
history
    ancient Japan (10,000 BCE–794 CE) 24–9
    Heian period (794–1185) 30–8
    Kamakura period (1185–1333) 39–44
    Nanbokucho/Muromachi period (1336–1573) 44–8
    Sengoku period (1467–1615) 51–7
    Edo period (1603–1868) 58–70
*hitatare* **128**
*hoate* 169
Hōgen Disturbance 36, **154**
Hōjo clan 39, 44, 45, 190, 198, 208
*hoko yari* 139
Hosokawa clan 48, **72**
hostage systems 204, 209

Ikkō sect 200, **204**
Imagawa clan 204, 206
Imagawa Yoshimoto 198, 199, 204
Imperial power
    *insei* 36, 44
    reunification of courts 48
    symbols and *mon* 214–15
    Tenji (Nakano Ōe) 28
iron 94, 100
iron-ore quality 74, 76, 86
Ito clan **220**

ji-samurai 48
*jinbaori* **52**, **98-9**, **220**
*jingasa* 171
*jingata* **109**
Jōmon period (c.10,000–c.300 BCE) 24–5

*kabuto* 105–10, 147–8, 170–2, **173**, **185**
    *see also* helmets
Kamakura period (1185–1333) 39–44
*kamishino* 126
*kamon* 215
*kara-bitsu* 132–3
*katana* **12**, 13, 16, 77, 88, 152, **153**
Kawanakajima, Battle of **50**, **56**, 191, **218**
*kawari-kabuto* 172, **173**
*keikō* 76, 141–4
*ken* 74
*kiku* 214–15
*kimono* 126

Kiyohara clan 35
*kobakama* 125
Kofun period (c.300–710) 27–30, **136**, 137
*kogake* 121–2
*kosodi* 125, 126
*kote* 119, **130**
*kozan-dō* 94–5
Kublai Khan 41, 42
*kusari* **158**, 159–60, **161**, **162**
*kusazuri* **112**, 118, **130**
*kyahan* 125

lacing 94, 101–3, 137, 176
lacquer 92, 95–6
lamellae 76, 92, 94, 96, 178
Later Three Years' War 35
leather 94, 98–100
leg protection 121–3, 142–4
loincloths 125

*mabizashi* 109, 147, 169
*mabizashi-tsuke kabuto* 148
Maeda clan **210**
Makino clan **220**
*manchira* **101**
*manju no wa* **100**
*maru-dō* 178
Matsudaira clan **213**
Meiji 66
*men yoroi* 105, 108–9, 166
*menpo* 105, 166–8, **185**
militia *see ashigaru*
Minamoto clan 35–9, **40**, **213**, **216**
Mito Rebellion **22**
*mogami-dō* 176, **177**
*mon* 211–21
Mongol forces 41–2, 97
*morohada-nugi-dō gusoku* 179
Muromachi period (1336–1573) 44–8

Nagao clan 190
*nagarebata* 221
Nagashino, Battle of **54**
*naginata* 14, 16, 90
*namban-dō* 181
*namban-kabuto* 171
Nanbokucho/Muromachi period (1336–1573) 44–8
Nara period (710–794) 30
*ni mai dō* 118
*nobori* 221
*nodawa* 166, **168**
*nodowa* **131**
*ō*-yoroi armour 77, **95**, 152–7
Oda clan **191**, 204
Oda Nobunaga 57, 58, **194**, 195, 197–200, **201**, 204, 206
odoshi-ge 102, 176
*okegawa-dō* 180
Okehazama, battles of 199
Ōnin War 48

Perry, Matthew 62–4, **65**
Portuguese traders 57, 80, **82**, 171, 181
protection of armour 19–20

riveting 94, 160, **162**, 180
*rokugu* 104
ronin 63
*rope sandals* 125

samurai
 famous **186**, 187–209
 Heian period 33–4
 ji-samurai 48
 meaning of word 8, 34
sandals 125, **127**
*sashimono* 217–18
Satsuma Rebellion 66, 86
scale armour 94–5, **102**, 141–4
Sekigahara, Battle of **207**
Sengoku period (1467–1615) 51–7
 famous samurai **186**, 187–209
*seppuku* 8–9
*shields* 116
*shikoro* 106–8, 118
Shintō 28
*shirts* 125
*shitagi* 125
shogunate 39, **40**, 44, 47–8, 66
*shokaku-tsuke kabuto* 148
*shomen* 168
shoulder guards **103**, 118, 121, 144, **146**
silk 81, 97–8, 126, 160
sleeves 119
slippers 125
*sode* 118, 121, **131**, **146**
Soga clan 28
*somen* 167
spears 14, **138**, 139, **213**
stingray skin **121**
*suneate* 122
surcoats **127**, **220**
swords
 Chinese **137**
 *daishō* 13, **16**
 fighting techniques 14–16
 *ken* 74
 Kofun period (c.300–710) 75, **79**
 metalworking skills and development 77, 88
 Nanbokucho/Muromachi period (1336–1573) 12

*tachi* 80
swordsmiths **153**
symbolism of armour 17–21

*tabi* 125
*tachi* 80
Taira clan **34**, **35**, 36–8
Takeda clan 198, **206**
Takeda Shingen 50, 188–94
*tankō* **75**, **76**, **92**, **137**, **138**, *141*
*tanto* **12**
tassets **112**, 118
*tatami dō* 113, **116**
*tateage* 122
*tekko* 119
Tenji (Nakano Ōe) 28, **29**, 30
throat protector 166, **168**
Tōgō Heihachirō 70
Tokugawa clan **191**
Tokugawa Ieyasu **55**, 58–61, **186**, 202–9
Tokugawa Yoshinobu 66
*tosei-gosuku* 175
Toyotomi Hideyoshi 58, **205**, 206–9
trade 24, 57, 61, 64, 74, **82**
transport of armour 119, 132–3
trousers 125
*tsuba* 74

Uesugi clan 190–4
Uesugi Kenshin 50, 191
underclothing 123–6, **128**

visors 148

*wakidate* 110
*wakizashi* **12**, 13
*waraji* 125, **127**
Warring States period (1467–1615) 51–7
weapons
 blades 14–16, 75–7, 88 *see also* swords
 bows 14, 77
 firearms 57, 80–1, 83

Yamamoto Kansuke **56**, **193**
Yamana clan 48
Yamato clan 27
*yari* 14, **138**, 139
Yayoi period (c.300 BCE–c.300 CE) 25–7
*yodare-kake* 166
*yoroi* **49**
*yumi* 14, 155

*zunari-kabuto* 172

# *Picture Credits*

Alamy: 5 &12 (World History Archive), 22 (History and Art Collection), 29 & 31 (CPA Media), 32 (World History Archive), 33 (Granger Historical Picture Archive), 37 (Science History Images), 40 (The Print Collector), 42 (Chronicle of World History), 43 (CPA Media), 45 (Heritage Image Partnership), 46 & 47 (Artgen), 54 (Science History Images), 56 (CPA Media), 64 (Penta Springs), 68/69 (Chronicle of World History), 78 & 79 (Leopold von Ungern), 80 (Tibbut Archive), 82 (Granger Historical Picture Archive),
87 (CPA Media), 93 (Interfoto), 94 (CPA Media), 95 (Granger Historical Picture Archive), 110 (Roger Bamber), 115 (Leopold von Ungern), 127 bottom left (PicoCreek), 134 (The Print Collector), 136 (Penta Springs), 138 left (Interfoto), 140 (Granger Historical Picture Archive), 141 (Leopold von Ungern), 155 (Granger Historical Picture Archive), 164 (Leopold von Ungern), 165 (Science History Images), 171 (Leopold von Ungern), 172 (XenLights), 178 (POL/BT), 183 & 185 (Interfoto), 189 & 193 (CPA Media), 197 (Interfoto),
203 (GL Archive), 207 (Classic Image), 216 (Havoc)

Amber Books: 128, 130, 131

Creative Commons Attribution 2.5 Generic License: 116 (Marie-Lan Nguyen)

Creative Commons Attribution License 4.0 International: 147 (Tokyo National Museum)

Creative Commons Attribution-Share Alike 2.0 France License: 139 (Rama)

Creative Commons Attribution-Share Alike 3.0 Unported License: 205 right (AlexHe34)

Dreamstime: 124 (Gallofoto), 188 (Yorozu Kitamura), 194 (Beibaoke1), 202 (Cowardlion)

Getty Images: 72 (Fine Art), 90 (De Agostini), 92 (Stan Honda), 119 (Werner Forman), 121 (Jacques Demarthon), 122 (De Agostini),
123 (Jacques Demarthon), 132 (Hulton Archive), 146 bottom & 159 (Werner Forman), 170 (Culture Club), 176 (Denver Post)

Getty Museum Collection (Creative Commons Attribution 4.0 International License): 174, 181 both, 182, 184

GNU Free Documentation License, Version 1.2: 100, 125 & 162 (Samuraiantiqueworld)

Library of Congress: 6, 9, 13, 15, 16, 34, 50, 63, 65, 150, 201

Los Angeles County Museum of Art: 35, 55, 86, 149, 154, 208, 212

Metropolitan Museum of Art, New York: 18 both, 20 all, 25, 26, 27, 30, 49 both, 52, 59, 74 both, 75, 77, 81, 84, 85, 88, 89, 96, 98, 99, 101, 102, 103, 105, 106, 107, 109, 111, 112, 113, 114, 117, 120, 126, 127 top left, 127 right, 133, 137, 138 right, 143, 145, 146 top, 148, 156, 157, 158, 163 both, 166, 167, 168, 169 both, 173, 177 both, 179, 180, 196, 198, 205 left, 210, 213 both, 214, 215, 220 all

Public Domain: 10, 11, 19, 21, 38, 39, 53, 60, 61, 66, 67, 70, 104, 142, 153, 161, 186, 191, 192, 195, 199, 200, 204, 206, 218/219

Shutterstock: 190 (yu_photo)

Walters Art Museum, Baltimore: 71, 152